A Voice of Warning

BY

Parley Parker Pratt

A VOICE OF WARNING AND INSTRUCTION TO ALL PEOPLE

CHAPTER I

ON PROPHECY ALREADY FULFILLED

We have also a more sure word of prophecy, whereunto ye do well that ye take heed as unto a light that shineth in a dark place, until the day dawn, and the day-star arise in your hearts: knowing this first, that no prophecy of the Scripture is of any private interpretation; for the prophecy came not in old time by the will of man, but holy men of God spake as they were moved upon by the Holy Ghost. — PETER.

In order to prove anything from Scripture, it is highly necessary in the first place to lay down some certain, definite, infallible rule of interpretation, without which the mind is lost in uncertainty and doubt, ever learning, and never able to come to the knowledge of the truth.

The neglect of such a rule has thrown mankind into the utmost confusion and uncertainty in all their biblical researches. Indeed, while mankind are left at liberty to transform, spiritualize, or give any uncertain or private interpretation to the word of God, all is uncertainty.

"Whatsoever was written aforetime, was written for our profit and learning, that we through patience and comfort of the Scriptures, might have hope." Now, suppose a friend from a distance should write us a letter, making certain promises to us on certain conditions, which, if we obtained, would be greatly to our profit and advantage: of course it might be said the letter was written for our profit and learning, that through patience and comfort of the letter we might have hope to obtain the things promised. Now if we clearly understood the letter, and knew what to expect, then it would afford us comfort and hope; whereas, if there was any doubt or uncertainty on our minds in the understanding of the same, then could we derive no certain comfort or hope from the things written, not knowing what to hope for; consequently the letter would not profit us at all. And so it is with the Scriptures. No prophecy or promise will profit the reader, or produce patience, comfort, or hope in his mind until clearly understood, that he may know precisely what to hope for. Now, the predictions of the Prophets can be clearly understood, as much so as the almanac when it foretells an eclipse; or else the Bible of all books is of most doubtful usefulness. Far better would it have been for mankind, if the great Author of our existence had revealed nothing to His fallen creatures, than to have revealed a book which would leave them in doubt and uncertainty, to contend with one another, from age to age, respecting the meaning of its contents. That such uncertainty and contention have existed for ages, none will deny. The wise and learned have differed, and do still widely differ, from each other, in the understanding of prophecy. Whence then this difference? Either Revelation itself is deficient, or else the fault is in mankind. But to say Revelation is deficient, would be to charge God foolishly; God forbid: the fault must be in man. There are two great causes for this blindness, which I will now show:

First, mankind have supposed that direct inspiration by the Holy Ghost was not intended for all ages of the Church, but was confined to primitive times; the "Canon of Scripture being full," and all things necessary being revealed; the Spirit which guides into all truth was no longer for the people: therefore they sought to understand, by their own wisdom, and by their own learning, what could never be clearly understood, except by the Spirit of Truth: for the things of God knoweth no man, except by the Spirit of God.

Secondly, having lost the Spirit of Inspiration, they began to institute their own opinions, traditions, and commandments; giving constructions and private interpretations to the written word, instead of believing the things written. And the moment they departed from its literal meaning, one man's opinion, or interpretation, was just as good as another's; all were clothed with equal authority, and from thence arose all the darkness and misunderstanding on these points, which have agitated the world for the last seventeen hundred years.

Among the variety of commodities which attract the attention of mankind, there is one thing of more value than all others. A principle which, if once possessed, will greatly assist in obtaining all other things worth possessing, whether it were power, wealth, riches, honors, thrones, or dominions. Comparatively few have ever possessed it, although it was within the reach of many others, but they were either not aware of it, or did not know its value. It has worked wonders for the few who have possessed it. Some it enabled to escape from drowning, while every soul who did not possess it was lost in the mighty deep. Others it saved from famine, while thousands perished all around them; by it men have often been raised to dignity in the state; yea, more, some have been raised to the throne of empires. The possession of it has sometimes raised men from a dungeon to a palace; and there are instances in which those that possessed it were delivered from the flames, while cities were consumed, and every soul, themselves excepted, perished. Frequently, when a famine or the sword has destroyed a city or nation, they alone who possessed it escaped unhurt. By this time the reader inquires, What can this be? Inform me, and I will purchase it, even at the sacrifice of all I possess on earth. Well, kind reader, this treasure is FOREKNOWLEDGE! a knowledge of things future! Let a book be published, entitled, "A Knowledge of the Future," and let mankind be really convinced that it did give a certain, definite knowledge of future events, so that its pages unfold the future history of the nations, and of many great events, as the history of Greece or Rome does unfold the past, and a large edition would immediately sell at a great sum per copy; indeed, they would be above all price. Now, kind reader, the books of the Prophets, and the Spirit of Prophecy were intended for this very purpose. Well did the Apostle say, "Covet earnestly the best gifts; but rather that ye prophesy."

Having said so much, we will now enter into the wide expanded field which lies before us, and search out the treasures of wisdom and knowledge which have been shining for ages like a light in a dark place. We will explore regions unknown to many; we will gaze upon the opening glories which present themselves on every side, and feast our souls with knowledge which is calculated in its nature to enlarge the heart, to exalt the mind, and to raise the affections above the little, mean, grovelling things of the world, and to make one wise unto salvation.

But, first, for the definite rule of interpretation. For this we will not depend on any man or commentary, for the Holy Ghost has given it by the mouth of Peter: "Knowing this first, that no prophecy of the Scripture is of any private interpretation." 2 Peter i, 20.

There is one grand division to be kept constantly, in view in the study of prophecy; namely, the distinction between the past and the future. The reader should be careful to ascertain what portion has been fulfilled, and what remains to be fulfilled: always remembering Peter's rule of interpretation will apply to both. Now, if we should find in our researches that every prophecy which has been fulfilled to the present year, has been literally fulfilled, then it follows of necessity that every prophecy which is yet future will not fail of a literal fulfilment. Let us commence with the days of Noah. Gen. vi, 17: "And behold I, even I, do bring a flood of waters upon the earth, to destroy all flesh, wherein is the breath of life, from under heaven; and every thing that is in the earth shall die."

In the verses which follow the above the Lord commands Noah to enter the Ark, and take with him animals of every kind, etc. And in the 22d verse it is written, "Thus did Noah, according to all that God commanded him, so did he." It was well for Noah that he was not well versed in the spiritualizing systems of modern divinity; for, under their benighted influence, he would never have believed that so marvelous a prophecy would have had a literal meaning and accomplishment. No, he would have been told that the flood meant a spiritual flood, and the Ark a spiritual Ark, and, the moment he thought otherwise, he would have been set down for a fanatic, knave, or fool; but it was so, that he was just simple enough to believe the prophecy literally. Here then is a fair sample of foreknowledge; for all the world, who did not possess it, perished by the flood.

The next prediction we will notice is Gen. xv, 13-16. "And he said unto Abraham. Know of a surety that thy seed shall be a stranger in a land that is not theirs, and shall serve them, and they shall afflict them four hundred years. And also that nation, whom they shall serve, will I judge; and afterwards shall they come out with great substance. And thou shalt go to thy fathers in peace; thou shalt be buried in a good old age; but in the fourth generation they shall come hither again, for the iniquity of the Amorites is not yet full."

The evil entreating of the children of Israel four hundred years, together with their coming out with great substance, and the judgment of God upon Egypt, as well as the death of Abraham in a good old age, are all facts too well known to need comment here; suffice it to say, that it is a striking example of the exact fulfilment of prophecy, uttered more than four hundred years before it had its accomplishment. From this we gather that none of those ancient men knew anything of the modern system of spiritualizing.

Our next is Gen. xix, 12, 13: "And the men said unto Lot, Hast thou here any besides? son-in-law, and thy sons, and thy daughters, and whatsoever thou hast in the city, bring them out of this place: for we will destroy this place, because the cry of them is waxed great before the face of the Lord; and the Lord hath sent us to destroy it." Now, Lot being simple enough to believe the thing in its literal sense, took as many of his family as would follow, and escaped for his life; to the great amusement, no doubt, of the Sodomites, who probably stood gazing after, crying "Delusion, delusion!" they thinking all the while that the prophecy was only a figure. Here is an example of a man escaping from the flames by foreknowledgeimparted to him, while the whole city perished. O! what a blessing that Lot had no knowledge of the modern manner of interpreting prophecy. If it had once entered his heart that he must come out of Sodom spiritually, instead of literally, it would have cost him his life.

Let us examine a prophecy of Joseph in the land of Egypt. Gen. xli, 29-31: "Behold, there come seven years of great plenty throughout all the land of Egypt: and there shall arise after them seven years of famine; and all the plenty shall be forgotten in the land of Egypt; and the famine shall consume the land: and the plenty shall not be known in the land by reason of that famine following; for it shall be very grievous." Joseph then proceeds to give directions for corn to be laid up in great abundance during the seven plenteous years, in order to provide against the famine. And

Pharaoh, being no better versed in the school of modern divinity than his predecessors, never once thought of any other interpretation but the most literal, And thus he was the means, together with Joseph, in the hand of God, of saving, not only their nation, but the house of Israel, from famine. This is another striking example of the power of foreknowledge. It not only saved from famine, but it exalted Joseph from a dungeon to a palace; from the lowest degradation to the highest honor; so that they cried before him, "Bow the knee!" But, O! what death and mourning would have followed had they dreamed only of spiritual famine and spiritual corn.

Having given a few plain examples of early ages, we will lightly touch upon some of the most remarkable events of prophecy, and its fulfilment, until we come down to the Jewish Prophets, where the field opens wide, touching in its progress the most remarkable events of all ages, and terminating in a full development of the opening glories of the last days.

One remarkable instance, concerning Elijah the Prophet, was, that he prophesied to Ahab that it should not rain for three years and upwards, which came to pass according to his word. There is also a remarkable instance of Hazael, the Syrian, who came to Elisha to inquire of the Lord concerning the king of Syria, his master, who was sick. The Prophet, earnestly beholding him, burst into tears: and Hazael asked him, saying, "Why weepest thou?" and he, answering, said, "The Lord hath showed me that thou shalt be king over Syria." And he then proceeded to unfold unto him the cruelties which he would afterwards exercise towards Israel, which are too horrible to mention here, lest in so doing I might offend the delicate ear. But Hazael, astonished to hear these things predicted concerning himself, which at that time filled him with horror, exclaimed with surprise, "But what? is thy servant a dog, that he should do this great thing?" Yet astonishing to tell, all was afterwards fulfilled to the very letter.

In the 21st chapter, 2 Chron., it is written that there came a writing to Jehoram from Elijah, which, after stating the great wickedness of which he had been guilty, in turning to idolatry, and also murdering his brethren of his father's house, who were better than himself, proceeds thus: "Behold, with a great plague will the Lord smite thy people, and thy children, and thy wives, and all thy goods; and thou shalt have great sickness by disease of the bowels, until thy bowels fall out, by reason of thy sickness, day by day." In the same chapter it is written, that the Philistines and Arabians came against him, and took his wives, and children, and goods captive; and after all this, the Lord smote him in his bowels with an incurable disease, and his bowels fell out by reason of his sickness, so he died of sore disease.

In the 6th chapter of Joshua, 26th verse, there is a wonderful prediction concerning Jericho: "Cursed be the man before the Lord, that riseth up and buildeth this city Jericho. He shall lay the foundation thereof in his first-born, and in his youngest son shall he set up the gates of it."

After this curse the city of Jericho lay waste for ages, none daring to rebuild it at the expense of their first-born and of their youngest son; until after a long succession of judges and kings, when hundreds of years had passed, Hiel the Bethelite, who lived in the days of Ahab, probably supposing that the Lord had forgotten the curse pronounced upon it by Joshua, ventured to rebuild the city: but no sooner had he laid the foundation thereof than Abiram his first-born died, and, still persevering in the hardness of his heart, he set up the gates thereof, with the loss of his youngest son, Segub, according to the word of the Lord by Joshua; see 1 Kings, xvi, 34. We might fill a volume with instances of a similar kind, dispersed through the historical part of the Scriptures; but we forbear, in order to hasten to a more full examination of the books of the Jewish Prophets. We shall trace them in their fulfilment upon Jerusalem, Babylon, Tyre, Egypt, and various other nations.

Babylon, the most ancient and renowned city of the world, was pleasantly situated on the banks of a majestic river, that flowed through the plains of Shinar, near to which the tower of Babel once stood. It was laid out four square, and surrounded with a wall upwards of three hundred feet high, and sixty miles in circumference; having a hundred gates of brass with bars of iron; twenty-five gates on each side, which opened to streets running through the city, a distance of fifteen miles; thus forming the whole city into exact squares of equal size. In the midst of these squares were beautiful gardens, adorned with trees and walks, diversified with flowers of varied hue; while the houses were built upon the borders of the squares, directly fronting on the streets. In the midst of this city sat Nebuchadnezzar, enthroned in royal splendor and magnificence, and swaying his sceptre over all the kingdoms of the world, when it pleased God, in a vision of the night, to unveil the dark curtain of the future, and to present before him, at one view, the history of the world, even down to the consummation of all things. Behold, a great image stood before him, whose head was of fine gold, his breast and arms of silver, his belly and thighs of brass, his legs of iron, his feet and toes part of iron and part of miry clay. He beheld, till a stone was cut out of the mountain without hands, which smote the image upon the feet, which were part of iron and part of clay, and brake them in pieces; then was the iron, the brass, the silver, and the gold, broken to pieces together, and became as the chaff of the summer threshing-floors; and the wind carried them away, and there was no place found for them; but the stone which smote the image became a great mountain, and filled the whole earth. When Daniel was brought in before the king, to tell the dream and the interpretation, he exclaimed, "There is a God in heaven that revealeth secrets, and maketh known to the king, Nebuchadnezzar, what shall be in the latter days." Then, after telling the dream, he continues thus: "Thou, O king, art a king of kings; for the God of heaven hath given thee a kingdom, power, and strength, and glory. And wheresoever the children of men dwell, the beasts of the field and the fowls of the heaven hath he given into thine hand, and hath made thee ruler over them all. Thou art this head of gold. And after thee shall arise another kingdom inferior to thee, and another third kingdom of brass, which shall bear rule over all the earth. And the fourth kingdom shall be strong as iron: forasmuch as iron breaketh in pieces and subdueth all things; and as iron that breaketh all these, shall it break in pieces and bruise. And whereas thou sawest the feet and toes, part of potters' clay, and part of iron, the kingdom shall be divided: but there shall be in it of the strength of the iron, forasmuch as thou sawest the iron mixed with miry clay. And as the toes of the feet werepart of iron, and part of clay, so the kingdom shall be partly strong, and partly broken. And whereas thou sawest iron mixed with miry clay, they shall mingle themselves with the seed of men: but they shall not cleave one to another, even as iron is not mixed with clay. And in the days of these kings shall the God of heaven set up a kingdom, which shall never be destroyed: and the kingdom shall not be left to other people, but it shall break in pieces and consume all these kingdoms, and it shall stand forever. Forasmuch as thou sawest that the stone was cut out of the mountain without hands, and that it brake in pieces the iron, the brass, the clay, the silver, and the gold; the great God hath made known to the king what shall come to pass hereafter; and the dream is certain, and the interpretation thereof sure."

In this great view of the subject we have presented before us, in succession, first, the kingdom of Nebuchadnezzar; second, the Medes and Persians, who took Babylon from Belshazzar, and reigned over all the earth; third, the Greeks under Alexander, who conquered the world, and reigned in the midst of Babylon; and fourth, the Roman empire, which subdued all things; fifth, its division into eastern and western empires, and its final breaking up or subdivision into the various kingdoms of modern Europe, represented by the feet and toes, part of iron and part of clay. And, lastly, we have presented before us an entirely new kingdom, organized by the God of heaven in the last days, or during the reign of these kings, represented by the feet and toes. This last kingdom was never to change masters, like all the kingdoms which had gone before it. It was never to be left to another people. It was to break in pieces all these kingdoms, and stand forever. Many suppose that this last kingdom alluded to was the kingdom of God which was organized in the days of Christ, or his Apostles. But a greater blunder could not exist; the kingdom of God set up in the days of Christ, or his Apostles, did not break in pieces any of the kingdoms of the world: it was itself warred against and overcome, in fulfilment of the words of

Daniel, chapter vii, 21; "I beheld, and the same horn made war with the saints, and prevailed against them;" also 22d verse, "Until the Ancient of Days came, and judgment was given to the saints of the Most High; and the time came that the saints possessed the kingdom;" also verse 27th, "And the kingdom and dominion, and the greatness of the kingdom, under the whole heaven, shall be given to the people of the saints of the Most High, whose kingdom is an everlasting kingdom; and all dominions shall serve and obey him."

John records, Rev. xiii. 7, "And it was given unto him to make war with the saints, and to overcome them; and power was given him over all kindreds, and tongues, and nations." In fulfilment of these sayings, power has been given, to the authorities of the earth to kill the Apostles and inspired men, until, if any remained, they were banished from among men, or forced to retire to the desolate islands, or the dens and caves of the mountains of the earth, being men of whom the world was not worthy; while at the same time, many false prophets and teachers were introduced in their place, whom men heaped to themselves, because they would not endure sound doctrine. In this way the kingdom of God became disorganized, and lost from among men, and the doctrines and churches of men instituted in its place. But we design to speak more fully on this subject when we come to treat on the subject of the kingdom of God. Suffice it to say, that the kingdom spoken of by Daniel is something to be organized in the last days, by the God of heaven Himself, without the aid of human institutions or the precepts of men. And, when once organized, it will never cease to roll; all the powers of earth and hell will not impede its progress, until at length the Ancient of Days shall sit, and the Lord Jesus will come in the clouds of heaven, with power and great glory, as the King of kings, and Lord of lords, and destroy all these kingdoms, and give the kingdom and the greatness of the kingdom, under the whole heaven, to the Saints. Then there will be but one Lord, and His name one, and He shall be King over all the earth.

We will now return to Nebuchadnezzar, whom the Lord, by the mouth of Jeremiah, calls His servant, to execute His judgment upon the nations. It seems that the Lord exalted this great man, and made him a king of kings, and lord of lords, arming him with His own sword, and clothing him with power and authority, for the express purpose of executing His judgments, and scourging and humbling all the nations of the earth. Jeremiah, chapter xxv, says that the Lord purposed to bring Nebuchadnezzar and his army against Jerusalem, and against all the nations round about, that he might bring them to desolation and captivity for seventy years; and after seventy years, He would turn and punish the king of Babylon and that nation for their iniquity. Now, who can trace the history of the fulfilment of these great events, so exactly pointed out by Jeremiah, Isaiah, and Ezekiel, and not be struck with astonishment and wonder at the marvellous gift of prophecy enabling men in those days to read the history of the future as they read the history of the past? Indeed, the reader of history in the nineteenth century, holding in his hand the history of the Babylonians, Medes and Persians, Greeks, Romans and Egyptians, together with that of the Jews, will hardly render himself more familiar with the events which transpired among those nations, than the Prophets were seventy years previous to their accomplishment.

The Jews were reduced to subjection by Nebuchadnezzar; their city, Jerusalem, was burned, together with their temple; their princes, nobles, and people were carried to Babylon, together with all their holy things. All the particulars of this destruction and captivity were distinctly foretold by Jeremiah, and the time of its continuance, viz., seventy years. After subduing the Jews, the king of Babylon marched his army against Tyre, the city of merchants, situated at the haven of the sea, surrounded not only by the sea, but by a strong wall. A hold so strong required the utmost skill and perseverance of Nebuchadnezzar and his whole army, who labored incessantly for a long time, and at length succeeded in taking Tyre, and bringing it into captivity for seventy years. After which they returned and established their city, for Jeremiah had previously foretold the reduction of Tyre, its captivity for seventy years, and its restoration at the expiration of that time. After the restoration of Tyre, the city flourished for a time, but was afterwards reduced to an entire desolation. Its ruined fragments are seen to this day in the bottom of the sea; its site has become a barren rock, only occupied by poor fishermen. All this desolation, and even its present appearance of desolation and perpetual waste, were clearly pointed out by the Prophets.

But when the king of Babylon had succeeded in taking Tyre, after many a bald head and peeled shoulder, caused by the hard service of his army in the siege, the Lord, by the mouth of Ezekiel, promised to give the spoils of Egypt unto him, for wages for his army, in order to pay him for the great service, wherewith he had served God, against Tyre. Next, witness his war in the taking of Egypt, and bringing it into captivity, until the seventy years were accomplished.

And, finally, trace him executing the Lord's vengeance and anger against Uz, upon the kings of the Philistines, and Askelon, Azaah; Ekrom, Edom, Moab, Ammon; Dedan, Tema, and Buz; and upon the kings of Arabia, Zimri and Elam; and upon all the kings of the Medes; and upon all the kings of the north, far and near; and finally upon all the kingdoms of the world, who were to be drunken, and spew, and fall to rise no more, because of the sword which He would send among them. But, when the Lord had accomplished all his mind on these nations, He purposed, in turn, to punish this great monarch, and those who succeeded him; and also the city and nation over which he reigned; and finally to make it perpetual desolations. And all this for their pride and haughtiness. The Lord exclaims: "Shall the ax boast itself against him that heweth therewith, or shall the saw boast itself against him that shaketh it?" etc. But, in order to trace the events of the return of the Jews, and the other nations, from their seventy years' captivity and bondage, and the punishment of Babylon, another and very different character from that of Nebuchadnezzar is introduced by the Prophets—one who is in Scripture termed the Lord's anointed. He may be considered one of the most extraordinary characters that ever the heathen world produced: his mildness, courage, perseverance, success, and, above all, his strict obedience to the command of that God which neither he nor his fathers had known, all go to prove that Isaiah was not mistaken when he called him by name, as the Lord's anointed, to deliver the nations from bondage, to scourge and subdue the greatest city and monarchy that have at any time existed on the earth, and to restore the Jews, and rebuild their city and temple. Indeed, he was one of those few whom the world never produces except for extraordinary purposes. But let us hear the Prophet's own description of him, Isaiah, chapter xlv: "Thus saith the Lord to his anointed, to Cyrus, whose right hand I have holden to subdue nations before him: and I will loose the loins of kings, to open before him the two-leaved gates, and the gates shall not be shut. I will go before thee, and make the crooked places straight: I will break in pieces the gates of brass, and cut in sunder the bars of iron. And I will give thee the treasures of darkness, and hidden riches of secret places, that thou mayest know that I, the Lord, which call thee by thy name, am the God of Israel. For Jacob my servant's sake, and Israel mine elect, I have even called thee by thy name: I have surnamed thee, though thou hast not known me. I am the Lord, and there is none else, there is no God beside me: I girded thee, though thou hast not known me: that they may know from the rising of the sun, and from the west, that there is none besides me." In the 13th verse, he says: "I have raised him up in righteousness, and I will direct all his ways: he shall build my city, and he shall let go my captives, not for price nor reward, saith the Lord of hosts." The reader will bear in mind that Isaiah lived about one hundred years before the Jewish captivity, and one hundred and seventy years before Cyrus caused their return.

Here I would pause and inquire, What power but the power of the great God could enable one man to call another by name, a century before his birth, and also to foretell correctly the history of his life? What must have been his wonder and astonishment, when, after many years of wars and commotions, during which he marched forth, conquering and to conquer, gathering as a nest the riches of the nations, he at last pitched his camp near the walls of the strongest hold in all the earth? He gazed upon its walls of upwards of three hundred feet in height, with its gates of brass and its bars of iron: the people within feeling perfectly safe, with provisions enough to last the inhabitants of the city for several years. How could he think of taking that city? Who would not have shrunk from such an undertaking, unless inspired by the great Jehovah? But, turning the river Euphrates from its course, and marching under the walls of the city, in the dried bed of the river, he found himself in possession of the city, without any difficulty; for Belshazzar, the king, was drinking himself drunk, with his nobles and concubines, and that, too, from the vessels of the House of the Lord which his father had taken from Jerusalem, and his knees had already smote together with horror, from the handwriting on the wall, which Daniel had just been called in to interpret, giving his kingdom to the Medes and Persians. Having subdued this great monarchy, he seated himself upon the throne of kingdoms; and, becoming familiar with Daniel, he was, no doubt, introduced to an acquaintance with the Jewish records, and then the mystery was unfolded: he could then see that God had called him by name, that the Almighty hand girded him for the battle, and directed all his work; he could then understand why the treasures of the earth poured themselves into his bosom, and why the loins of kings had been unloosed before him, and why the gates of brass had been opened, and the bars of iron burst asunder. It was that he might know that there was a God in Israel, and none else, and that all idols were as nothing; that he might also restore the Jews, and rebuild their city and temple, and fulfil God's purposes upon Babylon. He accordingly issued his proclamation to the Jews to return, and for the nations to assist them in rebuilding, "for," said he, "God hath commanded me to build him an house at Jerusalem." Ezra, chapter i, 2, 3, says: "Thus saith Cyrus, king of Persia, The Lord God of heaven hath given me all the kingdoms of the earth; and he hath charged me to build him an house at Jerusalem, which is in Judea. Who is there among you of all his people? his God be with him, and let him go up to Jerusalem, which is in Judea, and build the house of the Lord God of Israel, he is the God which is in Jerusalem."

What powerful argument, what mighty influence was it which caused Cyrus to be convinced that it was the God of heaven who dwelt at Jerusalem, who alone was God, and who had done all these things? He had not been traditioned in the belief of the true God, nor of the holy Scriptures. Nay, he had ever been very zealous in the worship of idols; it was to idols he looked for assistance in the former part of his life. I reply, it was the power of God, made manifest by prophecy and its fulfilment; not in a spiritualized sense, not in some obscure, uncertain, or dark, mysterious way, which was difficult to be understood; but in positive, literal, plain demonstration, which none could gainsay or resist. Isaiah says that this was the object the Lord had in view when he revealed such plainness. And Cyrus manifested that it had the desired effect.

I would here remark that when we come to treat of that part of prophecy which yet remains to be fulfilled, we shall bring proof positive that the heathen nations of the latter days are to be convinced in the same way that Cyrus was; that is, there are certain events plainly predicted in the Prophets, yet future, which, when fulfilled, will convince all the heathen nations of the true God, and they shall know that he hath spoken and performed it. And all the great and learned men of Christendom, and all societies, who put any other than a literalconstruction on the word of prophecy, shall stand confounded, and be constrained to acknowledge that all has come to pass even as it is written.

But to return to our research of prophecy and its fulfilment. The Prophets had not only predicted the reduction of Babylon by Cyrus, but they had denounced its fate through all ages, until reduced to entire desolation, never to be inhabited, not even as a temporary residence for the wandering Arab: "And the Arabian shall not pitch tent there." See Isaiah, xiii, 19-22.

Mr. Joseph Wolfe, the celebrated Jewish missionary, while traveling in Chaldea, inquired of the Arabs whether they pitched their tents among the ruins of Babylon, to which they replied in the negative, declaring their fears that, should they do so, Nimrod's ghost would haunt them. Thus all the predictions of the Prophets concerning that mighty city have been fulfilled.

Edom also presents a striking fulfilment of plain and pointed predictions in the Prophets. These predictions were pronounced upon Edom at a time when its soil was very productive and well cultivated, and everywhere abounding in flourishing towns and cities. But now its cities have become heaps of desolate ruins, only inhabited by the cormorant, bittern, and by wild beasts, serpents, etc., and its soil has become barren; the Lord has cast upon it the line of confusion, and the stones of emptiness, and it has been waste from generation to generation, in express fulfilment of the word of prophecy.

We will now give a passing notice of the vision of Daniel, recorded in the eighth chapter of his prophecies, concerning the ram and the goat. The reader would do well to turn and read the whole chapter; but we will more particularly notice the interpretation, as it was given him by Gabriel, recorded from the nineteenth to the twenty-fifth verses. And he said: "I will make thee know what shall be in the last end of the indignation, for at the time appointed the end shall be. The ram which thou sawest having two horns, are the kings of Media and Persia: and the rough goat is the king of Grecia; and the great horn that is between the eyes is the first king. Now that being broken, whereas four stood up for it, four kingdoms shall stand up out of the nation, but not in his power. And in the latter time of their kingdom, when the transgressors are come to the full, a king of fierce countenance, and understanding dark sentences, shall stand up; and his power shall be mighty, but not by his own power; and he shall destroy wonderfully, and shall prosper, and practise, and shall destroy the mighty and the holy people; and through his policy also he shall cause craft to prosper in his hand, and he shall magnify himself in his heart, and by peace shall destroy many; he shall also stand up against the Prince of princes; but he shall be broken without hand." In this vision we have first presented the Medes and Persians, as they were to exist until they were conquered by Alexander the Great. Now, it is a fact well known that this empire waxed exceedingly great for some time after the death of Daniel, pushing its conquests westward, northward, and southward, so that none could stand before it; until Alexander, the king of Grecia, came from the west, with a small army of chosen men, and attacked the Persians upon the banks of the river, and plunging his horse in, and his army following, they crossed, and attacked the Persians, who stood to oppose them on the bank with many times their number; but, notwithstanding their number, and their advantage of the ground, they were totally routed, and the Grecians proceeded to overrun and subdue the country, beating the Persians in a number of pitched battles, until they were entirely subdued. It is also well known that Alexander, the king of Greece, went forth from nation to nation, subduing the world before him, until, having conquered the world, he died at Babylon, at the age of thirty-two years. And thus, when he had waxed strong, the great horn was broken, and for it came up four notable ones towards the four winds of heaven. His kingdom was divided among four of his generals, who never attained unto his power. Now, in the latter time of their kingdom, when the transgression of the Jewish nation was come to the full, the Roman power destroyed the Jewish nation, took Jerusalem, caused the daily sacrifice to cease, and not only that, bat afterwards destroyed the mighty and holy people, that is, the Apostles and primitive Christians, who were slain by the authorities at Rome.

Now, let me inquire, Does the history of these United States give a plainer account of past events than Daniel's wisdom did of events which were then future, and some of them reaching down the stream of time for several hundred years, unfolding events which no human sagacity could possibly have foreseen? Man, by his own sagacity, may accomplish many things; he may plough the trackless ocean without wind or tide in his favor; he may soar aloft amid the clouds without the aid of wings; he may traverse the land with astonishing velocity without the aid of beasts; or he may convey his thoughts to his fellows by the aid of letters. But there is a principle which he can never attain to; no, not even by the wisdom of ages combined; money will not purchase it; it comes from God only, and is bestowed upon man as a free gift. Says the Prophet to the idols, "Tell us what shall be, thai we may know that ye are gods."

We will now proceed to show how exactly the prophecies were fulfilled literally in the person of Jesus Christ. "Behold," said the Prophet, "a virgin shall conceive and bear a son." Again, Bethlehem should be the place of his birth, and Egypt, where he sojourned with his parents, the place out of which he was to be called. He turned aside to Nazareth, for it was written, "He shall be called a Nazarene." He rode into Jerusalem upon a colt, the foal of an ass, because the Prophet had said, "Behold thy King cometh, meek and lowly, riding upon a colt," etc. And again, saith the Prophet: "He shall be afflicted and despised; he shall be a man of sorrows, and acquainted with grief; he shall be led as a lamb to the slaughter, and, like a sheep dumb before his shearers, so he opened not his mouth; in his humiliation his judgment was taken away; and who shall declare his generation, for his life is taken from the earth. He was wounded for our transgressions, and by his stripes we are healed; he was numbered with the transgressors; he made his grave with the rich." Not a bone of him is broken; they divide his raiment; cast lots for his vesture; give him gall and vinegar to drink; betray him for thirty pieces of silver; and finally, when it was finished, he rested in the tomb until the third day, and then rose triumphant, without seeing corruption. Now, kind reader, had you walked up and down with our dear Redeemer during his whole sojourn in the flesh, and had you taken pains to record the particular circumstances of his life and death, as they occurred from time to time, your history would not be a plainer one than the Prophets gave of him hundreds of years before he was born. There is one thing we would do well to notice concerning the manner in which the Apostles interpreted prophecy, and that is this—they simply quoted it, and recorded its literal fulfilment. By pursuing this course, they were enabled to bring it home to the hearts of the people in the Jewish synagogues, with such convincing proof that they were constrained to believe the supposed impostor whom they had crucified was the Messiah. But had they once dreamed of rendering a spiritualizing or uncertain application, like the teachers of the present day, all would have been uncertainty and doubt, and demonstration would have vanished from the earth.

Having taken a view of the Old Testament Prophets, concerning prophecy and its fulfilment, and having shown clearly that nothing but a literal fulfilment was intended, the objector may inquire whether the same mode will apply to the predictions contained in the New Testament. We will therefore bring a few important instances of prophecy, and its fulfilment, from the New Testament; after which we shall be prepared to enter the vast field which is still future. One of the most remarkable prophecies in sacred writ is recorded by Luke, chap, xxi, 20-24: "And when ye shall see Jerusalem compassed with armies, then know that the desolation thereof is nigh. Then let them which are in Judea flee to the mountains, and let them which are in the midst of it depart out; and let not them that are in the countries enter thereinto; for these be the days of vengeance, that all things which are written may be fulfilled. But woe unto them that are with child, and to them that give suck in those days; for there shall be great distress in the land, and wrath upon this people; and they shall fall by the edge of the sword, and shall be led away captive into all nations; and Jerusalem shall be trodden down of the Gentiles, until the times of the Gentiles be fulfilled." This prophecy involves the fate of Jerusalem and the temple, and the whole Jewish nation, for at least eighteen hundred years. About the year seventy, the Roman army compassed Jerusalem. The disciples remembered the warning which had been given them by their Lord and Master forty years before, and fled to the mountains. The city of Jerusalem was taken, after a long and tedious siege, in which the Jews suffered the extreme of famine, pestilence and the sword; filling houses with the dead, for want of a place to bury them, while women ate their own children, for want of all things. In this struggle there perished, in Judea, near one million and a half of Jews, besides those taken captive. Their country was laid waste, their city burned, their temple destroyed, and the miserable remnant dispersed abroad into all the nations of the earth; in which situation they have continued ever since, being driven from one nation to another, often falsely accused of the worst of crimes, for which they have been banished and their goods confiscated. Indeed, they have been mostly accounted as outlaws among the various nations; the soles of their feet have found no rest, and they have been a hiss and a byword; and people have said, "These are the people of the Lord, and are gone forth out of his land."

During all this time the Gentiles have possessed the land of Canaan, and trodden under foot the holy city where their forefathers worshipped the Lord. Now, in this long captivity, the Jews have never lost sight of the promises respecting their return. Their eyes have watched and failed with longing for the day, when they might possess again that blessed inheritance bequeathed to their forefathers; when they might again rear their city and temple, and re-establish their priesthood, and worship as in days of old. Indeed they have made several attempts to return, but were always frustrated in all their attempts; for it was an unalterable decree, that Jerusalem should be trodden down of the Gentiles, until the times of the Gentiles should be fulfilled. On the subject of this long dispersion, Moses and the Prophets have written very plainly; indeed, Moses even mentioned the particulars of their eating their children secretly in the siege and in the straitness, wherewith their enemies should besiege them in all their gates. Whoever will read the twenty-eighth of Deuteronomy, will read the history of what has befallen the Jews, foretold by Moses with all the clearness that characterizes the history of past events, and all this thousands of years before its accomplishment.

Our next is found in Acts xxi, 10, 11, where a Prophet named Agabus took Paul's girdle and bound his own hands and feet, and said: "Thus saith the Holy Ghost, So shall the Jews at Jerusalem bind the man that owneth this girdle, and shall deliver him into the hands of the Gentiles." The fulfilment of this prediction is too well known to need any description. We therefore proceed to notice a prophecy of Paul, recorded in 2 Tim. iv, 3, 4: "For the time will come, when they will not endure sound doctrine, but, after their own lusts, shall they heap to themselves teachers, having itching ears; and they shall turn away their ears from the truth, and shall be turned unto fables." This prophecy has been fulfilled to the very letter; for it applies to every religious teacher who has arisen from that day unto the present, except those commissioned by direct revelation and inspired by the Holy Ghost. But, to convince the reader of its full accomplishment, we need only point to the numberless priests of the day who preach for hire, and divine for money, and who receive their authority from their fellow man; and as to the fables to which they are turned, we need only to mention the spiritualizings and private interpretations which salute our ears from almost every religious press and pulpit.

But there is another prophecy of Paul well worth our attention, as illustrative of the times in which we live; it is found in the first five verses of the third chapter of 2 Timothy: "This know also that in the last days perilous times shall come; for men shall be lovers of their own selves, covetous, boasters, proud, blasphemers, disobedient to parents, unthankful, unholy, without natural affection, truce breakers, false accusers, incontinent, fierce, despisers of those that are good, traitors, heady, high minded, lovers of pleasures more than lovers of God, having a form of godliness, but denying the power thereof: from such turn away." From the last verse of this quotation we learn to our astonishment that this sum of awful wickednessapplies to professors of religion ONLY; that is, this would be the character of the (so called) Christian part of the community in the last days. Do not startle, kind reader; we do not make the application without proof positive to the point, for, remember, non-professors have no form of godliness, but those ungodly characters spoken of were to have a form of godliness, denying the power thereof. But, if you doubt Paul's testimony on the subject, look around you, examine for yourselves. "By their fruits ye shall know them." My heart is pained while I write. Alas, has it come to this; has the Spirit of Truth removed the veil of obscurity from the last days, only to present us with the vision of a fallen people; an apostate church, full of all manner of abominations, and even despising those who are good; while they themselves have nothing left but the form of godliness, denying the power of God; that is, setting aside the direct inspiration and supernatural gifts of the Spirit, which ever characterize the Church of Christ? Was it for this only that the Holy Spirit opened to the view of holy men the events of unborn time, enabling them to gaze upon the opening glories of the latter days? O ye Prophets and Apostles, ye holy men of old, what have you done if you stop here; if your prophetic vision only extended down the stream of time to the present year? Alas! you have filled our minds with sorrow and despair: the Jews you have left wandering in sorrow and darkness, far from all their hearts hold most dear on earth; their land a desolation, their city and temple in ruins, and they, without the knowledge of the true Messiah. The Gentiles, after partaking of the root and fatness of the tame olive tree, having fallen, after the same example of unbelief, are left without fruit, dead, plucked up by the roots, with naught but a form of godliness; while the powers that characterized the ancient church have fled from among men. Is this the consummation of all your labors? Was it for this you searched, toiled, bled, and died? I pause for a reply; if you have a word of comfort yet in store, concerning the future, let it quickly speak, lest our souls should linger in the dark valley of sorrow and despair!

CHAPTER II

ON THE FULFILMENT OF PROPHECY YET FUTURE

What is Prophecy but History reversed?

Having made the discovery and produced sufficient proof that the prophecies, thus far, have been LITERALLY fulfilled—to the very letter—we hope the reader will never lose sight of the same rule with regard to those yet future. And, while we stand upon the threshold of futurity, with the wonders of unborn time about to open upon our view, presenting before our astonished vision the most mighty and majestic scenes, the most astonishing revolutions, the most extraordinary destructions, as well as the most miraculous displays of the power and majesty of Jehovah, in His great restoration of His long dispersed covenant people from the four quarters of the earth: I say, as these scenes are about to open to our view, let us bow before the great I AM, in the name of Jesus, and pray in faith for His Spirit to enlarge our hearts and enlighten our minds, that we may understand and believe all that is written, however miraculous it may be. But, O! kind reader, whoever you are, if you are not prepared for persecution, if you are unprepared to have your name cast out as evil, if you cannot bear to be called a knave, an impostor, or madman, or one that hath a devil; or if you are bound by the creeds of men to believe just so much and no more, you had better stop here; for if you were to believe the things written in the Bible that are yet to come, you will be under the necessity of believing miracles, signs and wonders, revelations, and manifestations of the power of God, even beyond anything that any former generation has witnessed; yes, you will believe that the waters will be divided and Israel go through dryshod, as they journey to their own land, as they did in the days of Moses; for no man ever yet believed the Bible without believing and expecting such glorious events in the latter days. And I will now venture to say that a believer in the Bible would be something that very few men have ever seen in this generation, with all its boasted religion: for there is a great difference between believing the book to be true when shut, and believing the things therein written. It is now considered in Christendom a great disgrace not to believe the Bible when shut: but whosoever tries the experiment will find it a greater disgrace to believe that the things therein written will surely come to pass. Indeed, it is our firm belief in the things written in the Bible, and careful teaching of them, that is one great cause of the persecution we suffer. For let the prophecies be understood by the people, and let them roll on in their fulfilment, and this will blow to the four winds every religious craft in Christendom, and cause the kingdom of Christ to rise upon their ruins, while the actual knowledge of the truth will cover the earth as the waters do the sea.

Having said so much by way of caution, if there are any of my readers so bold, and regardless of consequences, as to dare with me to gaze upon the future, we will commence with Isaiah xi, 11, 12, 15, 16: "And it shall come to pass in that day, that the Lord shall set his hand again the second time to recover the remnant of his people, which shall be left, from Assyria, and from Egypt, and from Pathros, and from Cush, and from Elam, and from Shinar, and from Hamath, and from the islands of the sea. And he shall set up an ensign for the nations, and shall assemble the outcasts of Israel, and gather together the dispersed of Judah from the four corners of the earth. And the LORD shall utterly destroy the tongue of the Egyptian Sea; and with his mighty wind shall he shake his hand over the river, and shall smite it in the seven streams, and make men go over dryshod. And there shall be an highway for the remnant of his people, which shall be left from Assyria; like as it was to Israel in the day that he came up out of the land of Egypt."

Here you behold an ensign to be reared for the nations; not only for the dispersed of Judah, but the outcasts of Israel. The Jews are called dispersed, because they are scattered among the nations; but the ten tribes are called outcasts, because they are cast out from the knowledge of the nations, into a land by themselves. Now, the reader will bear in mind that the ten tribes have not dwelt in the land of Canaan since they were led captive by Shalmaneser, king of Assyria. We have also presented before us, in the fifteenth verse, the marvelous power of God, which will be displayed in the destruction of a small branch of the Red Sea, called the tongue of the Egyptian Sea; and also the dividing of the seven streams of some river, and causing men to go over dryshod; and, lest any should not understand it literally, the fifteenth verse says: "There shall be a highway for the remnant of his people, which shall be left from Assyria, like as it was to Israel when he came up out of the land of Egypt." Now, we have only to ask whether, in the days of Moses, the Red Sea was literally divided, or whether it was only a figure? For as it was then so shall it be again. And yet we are told by modern divines that the days of miracles have gone forever; and those who believe in miracles, in our day, are counted as impostors, or, at least, poor ignorant fanatics, and the public are warned against them, as false teachers who would, if possible, deceive the very elect. On the subject of this restoration the Prophets have spoken so fully and repeatedly, that we can only notice a few of the most striking instances, which will go to show the particular circumstances and incidents attending it, and the manner and means of its accomplishment. The sixteenth chapter of Jeremiah, fourteenth, fifteenth and sixteenth verses, says: "Therefore, behold, the days come, saith the Lord, that it shall no more be said, the Lord liveth that brought up the children of Israel out of the land of Egypt; but, the Lord liveth that brought up the children of Israel from the land of the north, and from all the lands whither he had driven them: and I will bring them again into their land that I gave unto their fathers. Behold, I will send for many fishers, saith the Lord, and they shall fish them; and after will I send for many hunters, and they shall hunt them from every mountain, and from every hill, and out of the holes of the rocks." Now it has ever been the case with Israel, when they wished to express the greatness of their God, to say, The Lord liveth, which brought up our fathers out of the land of Egypt. This saying at once called to mind the power and miracles of that memorable event, and associated with it all that was great and grand, and was calculated to strike the mind with awe, under a lively sense of the power of Israel's God. But, to our astonishment, something is yet to transpire which will cast into momentary forgetfulness all the great events of that day, and the children of Israel shall know that their God liveth, by casting their minds upon events of recent date, which shall have transpired, still more glorious and wonderful than their coming out of Egypt. They will exclaim, The Lord liveth, which recently brought the children of Israel from the north, and from all lands whither He had driven them, and hath planted them in the land of Canaan, which He gave our fathers. With this idea will be associated every display of grandeur and sublimity, of wonder and amazement; while they call to mind the revelations, manifestations, miracles and mercies displayed in bringing about this great event, in the eyes of all the nations. In view of this, Jeremiah exclaims, in the last verse of this chapter: "Therefore, behold, I will this once cause them to know, I will cause them to know mine hand and my might; and they shall know that my name is the Lord."

But the means made use of to bring about this glorious event are, not only the raising of a standard, the lifting up of an ensign, so that we may know when the time is fulfilled, but fishers and hunters are to be employed to fish and hunt them from every mountain, from every hill, and out of the holes of the rocks. Let the reader mark here: men were not to send missionaries, who were not inspired, to go and teach Israel several hundred different doctrines, and opinions of men, and to tell them they supposed the time had about arrived for them to gather; but the God of heaven is to call men by actual revelation, direct from heaven, and to tell them who Israel is; who the Indians of America are, if they should be of Israel; and also where the ten tribes are, and all the scattered remnants of that long lost people. He it is who is to give them their errand and mission, and to clothe them with power from on high to execute the great work, in defiance of opposing elements, and all the opposition of earth and hell combined. But do you ask: "Why is the Lord to commission men by actual revelation?" I reply, because He has no other way of sending men in any age. "No man," says the Apostle, "taketh this honor upon himself, but he that is called of God, as was Aaron." Now, we all acknowledge that Aaron was called by revelation.

Now the great Jehovah never did, nor never will, acknowledge the priesthood or ministry of any man who is not called by revelation, and inspired, as in days of old. But, "O!" says the reader, "you startle me, for the whole train of modern divines profess no revelation later than the Bible, and no direct inspiration or supernatural gift of the Spirit. Do you cast them all off, and say that they have no authority?" I reply, No, for the Bible does it, and I only humbly acquiesce in the decision, as they are nowhere known in the Scripture, except as teachers whom the people have heaped to themselves (the word heap does not mean a few, but many). But to prove more fully that God will give revelations in order to bring about this glorious work, we will refer you to Ezekiel xx, 33-38. It reads: "As I live, saith the Lord God, surely with a mighty hand, and with a stretched out arm, and with fury poured out, will I rule over you; and I will bring you out from the people, and will gather you out of the countries wherein ye are scattered, with a mighty hand, and with a stretched out arm, and with fury poured out. And I will bring you into the wilderness of the people, and there will I plead with you face to face. Like as I pleaded with your fathers in the wilderness of the land of Egypt, so will I plead with you, saith the Lord God, And I will cause you to pass under the rod, and I will bring you into the bond of the covenant, and I will purge out from among you the rebels, and them that transgress against me; I will bring them forth out of the country where they sojourn, and they shall not enter into the land of Israel; and ye shall know that I am the Lord."

You discover that this promise begins with a double assurance: first, with an oath, as I live; second, with an assurance, surely, with a mighty hand, etc. And, in the close of the same chapter, lest the people should possibly misunderstand him, he exclaims: "O Lord, they say of me, doth he not speak in parables?" Here we have the children of Israel brought from among all nations, with a mighty hand and a stretched out arm, and with fury poured out (O ye nations who oppose these things, beware, remember Pharaoh, and learn wisdom), we see them brought into the wilderness of the people; and there the Lord is to plead with them, face to face, just as he did with their fathers in the wilderness of Egypt. This pleading face to face can never be done without revelation, and a personal manifestation, as much so as in old times. Now I ask, were all His manifestations to Israel in the wilderness mere fables not to be understood literally? If so, this will be so too; for one will be precisely like the other, no parable, but a glorious reality. He will cause them to pass under the rod, and bring them into the bond of the covenant.

This brings to mind the new covenant so often promised in the Scriptures, to be made with the house of Israel and with the house of Judah, just in time to gather them from their long dispersion. Some may suppose that the new covenant which was to gather Israel made its appearance in the days of Christ and his Apostles. But Paul tells us it was yet future in his day. So, in his eleventh chapter to the Romans, he says, "that blindness in part is happened to Israel, until the fulness of the Gentiles be come in, and so all Israel shall be saved; as it is written, There shall come out of Sion the Deliverer, and shall turn away ungodliness from Jacob, for this is my covenant unto them, when I shall take away their sins." From this we learn that Paul placed that covenant in the future, even down to the restoration of Israel, in the last days, when the times of the Gentiles should be fulfilled. Then there should come a Deliverer for Israel, and not before, seeing that they had rejected the first coming of that Deliverer. And he himself said to the Jews: "Behold, your house is left unto you desolate; for I say unto you, ye shall not see me henceforth till ye shall say, Blessed is he that cometh in the name of the Lord." Then, and not until then, should the covenant be renewed with Israel. And even when the Apostles inquired, saying, "Wilt thou at this time restore again the kingdom to Israel?" the Savior made answer, that it was not for them to know the times and seasons which the Father had put in His own power; but they were to receive power, and bear witness of Him, etc.; as much as to say, that work is not for you Apostles to accomplish, but shall be done in the Lord's own time, by whom He will; but go ye and do the work I have commanded you.

Again, Isaiah, lxi, 8, 9, in speaking of this covenant, tells us that it should make their seed known among the Gentiles, and their offspring among the people; and should cause all that see them to acknowledge them that they are the seed that the Lord hath blessed. Now, we know that it is a question which can only be decided by revelation, whether the aborigines of America are the seed of Jacob or not. Again, it is a matter of uncertainty where the ten tribes are, or who they are; but the new covenant, whenever it makes its appearance, will reveal these things, and will leave the matter no longer in suspense; we shall then know their seed among the Gentiles, and their offspring among the people. But, O! how different was the effect of the covenant made eighteen hundred years ago in its effects upon Israel; it cast them off in unbelief, and caused all that have seen them or heard of them ever since to acknowledge that they are the seed that the Lord hath cursed. When the covenant is renewed in the last days, the Lord will bring them into the bond of the covenant, by manifesting Himself to them face to face. Let me inquire, How does God make a covenant with the people in any age? The answer is, By communicating His will to them by actual revelation; for, without this, it would be impossible to make a covenant between two parties. In order to illustrate this subject, let us bring an example. We see how we make covenants with each other. For instance, a young man wishes to enter into a covenant of matrimony with a young lady; but deprive him of the privilege of revealing his mind to her, cut off all direct communication between them, and a covenant could never be made; and so it is with the Almighty. He never did enter into a covenant with His creatures, without revelations; and He never can do it. In short, whenever He made a covenant with the people, where a whole people were concerned, He included in the covenant the priesthood, offices, and authorities, together with the ordinances and blessings which pertain to His covenant; and so will He do at this time. Whenever the new covenant is established, it will organize the kingdom of God with all its offices, ordinances, gifts, and blessings as in the days of old; but more of this when we come to treat of the kingdom of God.

"But," says the inquirer, "what need have we of the renewal of a covenant which has never been broken? If the Lord made a covenant in the days of the Apostles, called a new covenant, why should that covenant still be renewed again, seeing it is in full force, until it is broken by one party or the other?" This is an important inquiry, involving the fate of all Christendom in its decision; we must therefore be very careful to make the decision perfectly plain, and the proof easy to be understood. That there was a covenant made between God and the people in the days of Christ and His Apostles, none will attempt to deny, and if that covenant never has been broken, it must be of force to the present day, and consequently there is no need of a new one. It therefore remains for us to prove that that covenant has been broken, completely broken, so that it is not in force, either among Jews or Gentiles, having lost its offices, authorities, powers, and blessings, insomuch that they are nowhere to be found among men. In order to do this, we must examine what were its offices, authorities, powers, and blessings, and then see whether they are still known among men.

We read that its offices consisted of Apostles, Prophets, Evangelists, Pastors, and Teachers, all inspired and set in the Church, by the Lord Himself, for the edifying of the saints, for the work of the ministry, etc. And they were to continue in the Church, wherever it was found, until they all came to the unity of the faith, and unto the measure of the stature of a man in Christ.

Secondly, the gifts of the Spirit, which some call supernatural, were the powers and blessings which pertained to that covenant, wherever it existed, among the Jews or the Gentiles, so long as the covenant was of force. Now, I would ask the world of Christendom, or either of its sects or parties, if they have Apostles, Prophets, Evangelists, Pastors and Teachers inspired from on high, together with all the gifts and blessings of the Holy Spirit, which pertained to the Gospel covenant? If not, then the offices and powers of that covenant have been lost. And it must be through the breaking of that covenant that they were lost, for in this way the Jews lost these privileges, when they were handed to the Gentiles. And Paul told the Gentiles, in his eleventh chapter to the Romans, that if they did not abide in the goodness of God, they would fall, as the Jews had done before them.

But in order to prove, by further demonstration, that the Gospel covenant has been broken, by Jew and Gentile, and all people, so as to be no longer in force, I shall quote Isaiah, xxiv, 1-6: "Behold, the Lord maketh the earth empty, and maketh it waste, and turneth it upside down, and scattereth abroad the inhabitants thereof. And it shall be, as with the people, so with the priest; as with the servant, so with his master; as with the maid, so with her mistress; as with the buyer, so with the seller; as with the lender, so with the borrower; as with the taker of usury, so with the giver of usury to him. The land shall be utterly emptied, and utterly spoiled: for the Lord hath spoken this word. The earth mourneth and fadeth away, the world languisheth and fadeth away, the haughty people of the earth do languish. The earth also is defiled under the inhabitants thereof; BECAUSE THEY HAVE TRANSGRESSED THE LAWS, CHANGED THE ORDINANCE, BROKEN THE EVERLASTING COVENANT. Therefore hath the curse devoured the earth, and they that dwell therein are desolate: therefore the inhabitants of the earth are burned, and few men left." In these few verses, we discover a like calamity awaiting priests and people, rich and poor, bond and free, insomuch that they are all to be burned up but a few; and the complaint is that the earth is defiled under the inhabitants thereof, because they have transgressed the laws, changed the ordinance, and broken the everlasting covenant. Now this could not be speaking of any other than the covenant, ordinance, and laws of the Gospel, made with the people in the days of the Apostles; because, however any former covenant may have been broken, yet the inhabitants of the earth have never been destroyed by fire, all but a few, for having broken any previous covenant. But this destruction is to come by fire, as literally as the flood in the days of Noah; and it will consume both priests and people from the earth, and that, too, for having broken the covenant of the Gospel, with its laws and its ordinances; or else we must get a new edition of the Bible, leaving out the twenty-fourth of Isaiah.

Now, having settled this question, I trust the reader will see the need of a new covenant, in order to save the few that are not to be burned. We will therefore drop this subject for the present, and turn again to the subject of the gathering of Israel. You will please turn and read the thirty-sixth, thirty-seventh, thirty-eighth, and thirty-ninth chapters of Ezekiel. In the thirty-sixth chapter you will discover a promise that Israel are to return from all the nations whither they have been scattered, and to be brought again to the land which God gave to their fathers; Jerusalem is to be filled with flocks of men, and all the desolate cities of Judea are to be rebuilt, fenced and inhabited; the land is to be fenced, tilled and sown, insomuch that they shall say: "This land that was desolate is become like the garden of Eden." "I the Lord have spoken it, and I will do it; and the heathen shall know that I the Lord build the ruined places, and plant that that was desolate." "So shall the waste cities be filled with flocks of men, and they shall know that I am the Lord." In the thirty-seventh chapter you will find, after the vision of the resurrection of the dead, the Prophet goes on to speak of the two nations becoming one nation upon the mountains of Israel, and one king being king to them all; and when this takes place, they are no more to be divided into two kingdoms. Moreover, the Lord's tabernacle is to be with them, and His sanctuary in the midst of them forevermore. He will forever be their God, and they shall be His people. "And the heathen shall know that I the Lord do sanctify Israel, when my sanctuary shall be in the midst of them forevermore." Now, it is a fact well known, that Judah and the ten tribes have never been one nation, upon the mountains of Israel, since the day they were first divided into two nations.

But, when this does take place, even the very heathen are to know it, and are to be convinced of the true God, as was Cyrus. Now if the missionaries should convert the world, before the Lord does this great work, then it will save the Lord the trouble of doing it in His own way, and it will save the trouble of fulfilling the Prophets, and the word of the Lord will fail, and all the world lay hold of infidelity. Well did the Lord say: "My ways are not as your ways, nor my thoughts as your thoughts." Chapters xxxviii and xxxix present us with a view of many nations united under one great head, whom the Lord is pleased to call Gog; and being mounted on horseback, and armed with all sorts of armor, they come up against the mountains of Israel, as a cloud to cover the land; their object is to take a prey, to take away silver and gold, and cattle, and goods in great abundance.

This is an event which is to transpire after the return of the Jews, and the rebuilding of Jerusalem; while the towns and the land of Judea are without walls, having neither bars nor gates. But while they are at the point to swallow up the Jews, and lay waste their country, behold the Lord's fury comes up in His face, a mighty earthquake is the result, insomuch that the fishes of the sea, and the fowls of the air, and all the creeping things, and all men upon the face of the earth, shall shake at His presence, and every wall shall fall to the ground, and every man's sword shall be turned against his neighbor in this army, and the Lord shall rain upon Gog, and upon his bands, and upon the many people that are with him, an overflowing rain, great hailstones, fire and brimstone. And thus He will magnify Himself, and sanctify Himself, in the eyes of many nations, and they shall know that He is the Lord; thus they shall fall upon the open field, upon the mountains of Israel, even Gog and all his army, horses and horsemen; and the Jews shall go forth and gather the weapons of war, such as handstaves, spears, shields, bows and arrows; and these weapons shall last the cities of Israel seven years for fuel, so that they shall cut no wood out of the forest, for they shall burn the weapons with the fire; and they shall spoil those that spoiled them, and rob those that robbed them, and they shall gather gold and silver, and apparel, in great abundance.

At this time the fowls of the air, and the beasts of the field shall have a great feast; yea, they are to eat fat until they be full, and drink blood until they be drunken. They are to eat the flesh of captains, and kings, and mighty men, and all men of war. But the Jews will have a very serious duty to perform, which will take no less than seven months; namely, the burying of their enemies. They will select a place on the east side of the sea, called the Valley of the Passengers, and there shall they bury Gog and all his multitude, and they shall call it the Valley of Hamon Gog. And the scent shall go forth, insomuch that it shall stop the noses of the passengers; thus shall they cleanse the land. "And I will set my glory among the heathen, and all the heathen shall see my judgment that I have executed, and my hand that I have laid upon them: so the house of Israel shall know that I am the Lord their God from that day and forward. And the heathen shall know that the house of Israel went into captivity for their iniquity; because they trespassed against me, therefore hid I my face from them, and gave them into the hand of their enemies; so fell they all by the sword. According to their uncleanness, and according to their transgressions, have I done unto them, and hid myself from them. Therefore thus saith the Lord God, Now will I bring again the captivity of Jacob, and have mercy upon the whole house of Israel, and will be jealous for my holy name: after that they have borne their shame, and all their trespasses whereby they have trespassed against me, when they dwelt safely in their own land, and none made them afraid. When I have brought them again from the people, and gathered them out of their enemy's lands, and am sanctified in them in the sight of many nations; then shall they know that I am the Lord their God, which caused them to be led into captivity among the heathen; but I have gathered them into their own land, and have left none of them any more there. Neither will I hide my face any more from them; for I have poured out my Spirit upon the house of Israel, saith the Lord God."

In the foregoing, we discover that the heathen are to know that the house of Israel went into captivity for their iniquity, and are gathered again by the hand of God, after having borne their shame for all their trespasses: and the house of Israel will know that it was the Lord their God who caused them to be led into captivity among the heathen, and that He it was that gathered and defended them, and He will hide His face no more from them, but will pour out His Spirit upon them.

O ye blind, ye stiffnecked, ye hardhearted generation, with the Bible circulated among all nations, will whole nations be so blind as to fulfil this prophecy, and not know it until it brings destruction upon their own heads? Why all this blindness? Alas! it is because of false teachers, who will tell them the Bible must be spiritualized. Others declare that these prophecies can never be understood until they are fulfilled. If this be the case, then we can never escape the judgments predicted in them, but must continue the children of darkness, until they come upon us unawares and sweep us from the earth. Then, where will be the consolation of looking back and seeing them fulfilled? But blessed be God, He has told us by the mouth of Daniel that many shall run to and fro, and knowledge shall be increased, and that the wise shall understand, but none of the wicked shall understand. And now, I would ask, who are more wicked than the wilfully blind leaders of the blind, who tell us we cannot understand the Scriptures?

Zachariah, in his fourteenth chapter, has told us much concerning the great battle and overthrow of the nations who fight against Jerusalem; and he has said, in plain words, that the Lord shall come at the very time of the overthrow of that army; yes, in fact, even while they are in the act of taking Jerusalem, and have already succeeded in taking one half the city, and spoiling their houses, and ravishing their women. Then, behold their long expected Messiah, suddenly appearing, shall stand upon the Mount of Olives, a little east of Jerusalem, to fight against those nations and deliver the Jews. Zachariah says, The Mount of Olives shall cleave in twain, from east to west, and one half of the mountain shall remove to the north, while the other half falls off to the south, suddenly forming a very great valley, into which the Jews shall flee for protection from their enemies, as they fled from the earthquake in the days of Uzziah, king of Judah; while the Lord cometh and all the saints with him. Then will the Jews behold that long, long expected Messiah, coming in power to their deliverance, as they always looked for Him. He will destroy their enemies, and deliver them from trouble at the very time they are in the utmost consternation, and about to be swallowed up by their enemies.

But what will be their astonishment, when they are about to fall at the feet of their Deliverer, and acknowledge him their Messiah! They discover the wounds which were once made in his hands, feet, and side; and, on inquiry, at once recognize Jesus of Nazareth, the king of the Jews, the man so long rejected. Well did the Prophet say, they should mourn and weep, every family apart, and their wives apart. But, thank heaven, there will be an end to their mourning; for He will forgive their iniquities, and cleanse them from all uncleanness. Jerusalem shall be a holy city from that time forth, and all the land shall be turned as a plain from Geba to Rimmon, and she shall be lifted up and inhabited in her place, and men shall dwell there, and there shall be no more utter destruction of Jerusalem; "and in that day there shall be one Lord, and His name one, and He shall be King over all the earth."

John, in his eleventh chapter of Revelations, gives us many more particulars concerning this same event. He informs us that, after the city and temple are rebuilt by the Jews, the Gentiles will tread it underfoot forty and two months, during which time there will be two Prophets continually prophesying and working mighty miracles. And it seems that the Gentile army shall be hindered from utterly destroying and overthrowing the city, while these two Prophets continue. But, after a struggle of three years and a half, they at length succeed in destroying these two Prophets, and then overrunning much of the city; they send gifts to each other because of the death of the two Prophets, and in the mean time will not allow their dead bodies to be put in graves, but suffer them to lie in the streets of Jerusalem three days and a half; during which the armies of the Gentiles, consisting of many kindreds, tongues, and nations, passing through the city, plundering the Jews, see their dead bodies lying in the street. But, after three days and a half, on a sudden, the spirit of life from God enters them, and they will arise and stand upon their feet, and great fear will fall upon them that see them. And then they shall hear a voice from heaven, saying, "Come up hither," and they will ascend up to heaven in a cloud, their enemies beholding them. And, having described all these things, then come the shaking, spoken of by Ezekiel, and the rending of the Mount of Olives, spoken of by Zachariah. John says: "The same hour there was a great earthquake, and the tenth part of the city fell; and in the earthquake were slain of men seven thousand." And then one of the next scenes that follow is the sound of voices, saying: "The kingdoms of this world are become the kingdoms of our Lord and of His Christ, and He shall reign forever and ever."

Now, having summed up the description of these great events spoken of by these Prophets, I would just remark, there is no difficulty in understanding them all to be perfectly plain and literal in their fulfilment.

Suffice it to say, the Jews gather home, and rebuild Jerusalem. The nations gather against them to battle. Their armies encompass the city, and have more or less power over it for three years and a half. A couple of Jewish Prophets, by their mighty miracles, keep them from utterly overcoming the Jews; until at length they are slain, and the city is left in a great measure to the mercy of their enemies for three days and a half; the two Prophets rise from the dead and ascend up into heaven. The Messiah comes, convulses the earth, overthrows the army of the Gentiles, delivers the Jews, cleanses Jerusalem, cuts off all wickedness from the earth, raises the saints from the dead, brings them with Him, and commences His reign for a thousand years; during which time His Spirit will be poured out upon all flesh; men and beasts, birds and serpents, will be perfectly harmless, and peace and the knowledge and glory of God shall cover the earth as the waters cover the sea; and the kingdom, and the greatness of the kingdom under the whole heaven, shall be given to the saints of the Most High.

During this thousand years, Satan will be bound, and have no power to tempt the children of men. And the earth itself will be delivered from the curse, which came by reason of the Fall. The rough places will become smooth, the barren deserts fruitful;

the mountains leveled; the valleys exalted; the thorn and thistle shall no more be found, but all the earth shall yield her increase in abundance to the saints of God. But, after the thousand years are ended, then shall Satan be loosed, and shall go out to deceive the nations which dwell in the four quarters of the earth, to gather them to battle, and to bring them up to battle against the camp of the saints. Then the great and last struggle shall take place between God and Satan, for the empire of the earth. Satan and his army shall be overthrown. And after these great things, come the end of the earth, the resurrection of the wicked, and the last judgment. And there shall be a new earth and a new heaven, for the former earth and the former heaven shall have passed away, that is, they will be changed from temporal to eternal, and made fit for the abode of immortals. Then cometh Jerusalem down from God, out of heaven, having been renewed as well as the heavens and the earth. "For," says He, "behold, I make all things new."

This new city, placed upon the new earth, with the Lord God and the Lamb in the midst, seems to be man's eternal abode, insomuch that, after all our longings for a place beyond the bounds of time and space, as saith the poet, we are at last brought to our proper senses, and given to understand that man is destined forever to inherit this selfsame planet, upon which he was first created, which shall be redeemed, sanctified, renewed, purified, and prepared as an eternal inheritance for immortality and eternal life; with the holy city for its capital, the throne of God in the midst, for its seat of government; and watered with a stream, clear as crystal, called the Waters of Life, issuing from the throne of Jehovah; while either side is adorned with trees of never fading beauty. "Blessed are they that do his commandments, that they may have a right to the tree of life, and may enter in through the gates into the city." By this time we begin to understand the words of the Savior: "Blessed are the meek, for they shall inherit the earth." And also the song which John heard in heaven, which ended thus: "We shall reign on the EARTH."

Reader, do not be startled; suppose you were to be caught up into heaven, there to stand with the redeemed of every nation, kindred, tongue, and people, and join them in singing, and to your astonishment, all heaven is filled with joy, while they tune the immortal lyre, in joyful anticipation of one day reigning on the earth — a planet now under the dominion of Satan, the abode of wretchedness and misery, from which your glad spirit had taken its flight, and, as you supposed, an everlasting farewell. You might perhaps be startled for a moment, and inquire within yourself: "Why have I never heard this theme sung among the churches on earth?" Well, my friend, the answer would be — "Because you lived in a day when people did not understand the Scriptures."

Abraham would tell you, you should have read the promise of God to him, Gen. xvii, 8, where God not only promised the land of Canaan to his seed for an everlasting possession, but also to him. Then you should have read the testimony of Stephen, Acts, vii, 5, by which you would have ascertained that Abraham never had inherited the things promised, but was still expecting to rise from the dead and be brought into the land of Canaan, to inherit them. "Yes," says Ezekiel, "if you had read the thirty-seventh chapter of my prophecies, you would have found a positive promise, that God would open the graves of the whole house of Israel, who were dead, and gather up their dry bones, and put them together, each to its own proper place, and even clothe them again with flesh, sinews, and skin, and put His Spirit in them, and they should live; and then, instead of being caught up to heaven, they should be brought into the land of Canaan, which the Lord gave them, and they should inherit it."

But, still astonished, you might turn to Job; and he, surprised to find one unacquainted with so plain a subject, would exclaim: "Did you never read my nineteenth chapter, from the twenty-third to the twenty-seventh verses, where I declare, I wish my words were written in a book, saying, that my Redeemer would stand on the earth in the latter-day; and that I should see Him in the flesh, for myself, and not another; though worms should destroy this body?" Even David, the sweet singer of Israel, would call to your mind the thirty-seventh Psalm, where he repeatedly declares that the meek shall inherit the earth forever, after the wicked are cut off from the face thereof.

And last of all, to set the matter forever at rest, the voice of the Savior would mildly fall upon your ear, in his sermon on the mount, declaring emphatically: "Blessed are the meek, for they shall inherit the earth." To these things you would answer: "I have read these passages, to be sure, but was always taught to believe that they did not mean so, therefore, I never understood them until now. Let me go and tell the people what wonders have opened to my view, since my arrival in heaven, merely from having heard one short song. It is true, I have heard much of the glories of heaven described, while on earth, but never once thought of their rejoicing in anticipation of returning to the earth." Says the Savior: "They have Moses and the Prophets; if they will not believe them, neither would they believe although one should rise from the dead."

We will now return to the subject of the coming of Messiah, and the ushering in of that glorious day, called the Millennium, or rest of a thousand years. We gather from the field of prophecy, through which we have passed: first, that that glorious day will be ushered in by the personal coming of Christ, and the resurrection of all the saints; second, that all the wicked will be destroyed from the earth, by overwhelming judgments of God, and by fire, at the time of His coming, insomuch that the earth will be cleansed by fire from its wicked inhabitants, as it once was by water; and this burning will include priests as well as people: all but a few shall be burned. This burning more especially applies to the fallen church, rather than to the heathen or Jews, whom they are now trying to convert. Woe unto you, Gentiles, who call yourselves the people of the Lord, but have made void the law of God by your traditions; for in vain do you call Lord, Lord, and do not the things which Jesus commands; in vain do ye worship Him, teaching for doctrines the commandments of men. Behold, the sword of vengeance hangs over you, and except you repent, it will soon fall upon you; and it will be more tolerable in that day for the Jews and heathen than for you. Behold, ye flatter yourselves that the glorious day spoken of by the Prophets will be ushered in by your modern inventions and moneyed plans, which are got up in order to convert the Jews and heathen to the various sectarian principles now existing among yourselves; and you expect, when this is done, to behold a millennium after your own heart. But the Jews and heathen never will be converted, as a people, to any other plan than that laid down in the Bible for the great restoration of Israel. And you yourselves are laboring under a broken covenant, and ripening for the fire as fast as possible. But do not count me your enemy because I tell you the truth, for God is my witness that I love your souls too well to keep back any truth from you, however severe it may seem. The wounds of a friend are better than the kisses of an enemy. Now, concerning the signs of the times, the inquiry often arises: "When shall these things be, and what signs shall there be when these things shall come to pass?" I am often asked the question, whether it is near at hand; I will therefore tell you all, whereby you may know for yourselves when it is nigh, even at the doors, and not be dependent on the knowledge of others.

Now, you behold the apple tree, and all the trees, when they begin to shoot forth their leaves, ye know of your own selves that summer is nigh at hand; and so likewise when ye shall see great earthquakes, famines, pestilence, and plagues of every kind; the sea breaking beyond its bounds, and all things in commotion; the nations distressed with perplexity; men's hearts failing them for fear, and for looking for the things which are coming on the earth; when you see signs in the heaven above, and in the earth beneath, blood, and fire, and vapor of smoke, the sun turned to darkness, the moon to blood, and stars hurled from their courses; when you see the Jews gathering to Jerusalem, and the armies of the nations gathering against them to battle, you may know, with a perfect knowledge, that Christ's coming is near, even at the doors. "Verily, I say unto you, this generation shall not pass till all these things be fulfilled." Heaven and earth shall pass away, but not one word of all that the Lord has spoken by the mouth of His holy Prophets and Apostles shall fail.

Whoever will look to the word of the Prophets, and to the sayings of Jesus Christ, on this subject, the same will be convinced that all the signs of which I have spoken are clearly pointed out as the signs of His coming. But, notwithstanding all these things are written, His coming will overtake the world unawares, as the flood did the people in the days of Noah. The reason is, they will not understand the Prophets. They will not endure sound doctrine; their ears are turned away from the truth, and turned to fables, because of false teachers, and the precepts of men; and what is still worse, when God sends men with the New and Everlasting Covenant, and clothes them with boldness to testify to the truth, they will be treated as the servants of God have been before them by the fallen churches; every church will cleave to its own way, and will unite in saying: "There is no need of these new things, the good old way is right;" while at the same time they are walking in as many different ways as there are sects, and only agree in persecuting and speaking all manner of evil against the fishers and hunters whom God shall send. But, thank heaven, there are individuals in every sect who are humbly seeking the truth, and who will know the voice of truth, and be gathered out, and planted in the New and Everlasting Covenant; and they will be adopted into the family of Israel, and will be gathered with them, and be partakers of the same covenant of promise. Yea, as Jeremiah says, in the sixteenth chapter of his Prophecies: "The Gentiles shall come unto thee from the ends of the earth, and shall say, surely our fathers have inherited lies, vanities, and things wherein there is no profit." But as the Jews overlooked Christ's first coming, by not understanding the Prophets, and fastening their whole expectations on His glorious coming in the last days, to restore the kingdom to Israel, and avenge them of their enemies, and, by this mistake, were broken and scattered; so the Gentiles will overlook the prophecies concerning His second coming, by confounding them with the last judgment, which is to take place more than a thousand years afterward. But this fatal mistake, instead of causing the Gentiles to be broken and scattered, will cause them to be ground to powder.

O my brethren, according to the flesh, my soul mourns over you, and had I a voice like a trumpet, I would cry, Awake, awake and arouse from your slumber, for the time is fulfilled, your destruction is at the door, "for I have heard from the Lord God of Hosts, a consumption, even determined upon the whole earth!" Prepare to meet your God I And again, Awake, O house of Israel, and lift up your heads, for your redemption draweth nigh: yea, depart ye, depart ye, go ye out from hence, gather home from your long dispersion, rebuild your cities; yea, go ye out from the nations, from one end of heaven to the other; but let not your flight be in haste, for the Lord shall go before you, and the God of Israel shall be your rearward! And finally, I would say to all, both Jew and Gentile, Repent ye, repent ye, for the great day of the Lord is at hand; for if I, who am a man, do lift up my voice, and call upon you to repent, and ye hate me, what will ye say when the day cometh, when the thunders shall utter their voices to the ends of the earth, speaking to the ears of all that live, saying: "Repent, and prepare for the great day of the Lord?" Yea, again, when the lightnings shall streak from the east unto the west, and shall utter forth their voices unto all that live, and make the ears of all that hear to tingle, saying these words: "Repent ye, for the great day of the Lord is come?" And again, the Lord shall utter His voice out of heaven, saying: "Hearken, O ye nations of the earth, and hear the words of that God who made you: O ye nations of the earth, how oft would I have gathered you together as a hen gathereth her chickens under her wings, but ye would not! How often have I called upon you by the mouth of my servants, and by the ministering of angels, and by mine own voice, and by the voice of thunderings, and by the voice of lightnings, and by the voice of tempests, and by the voice of earthquakes and great hailstorms, and by the voice of famine and pestilences of every kind, and by the great sound of a trumpet, and by the voice of judgments, and by the voice of mercy, all the day long, and by the voice of glory and honor, and the riches of eternal life, and would have saved you with an everlasting salvation, but you would not! Behold, the day has come, when the cup of the wrath of mine indignation is full."

CHAPTER III

THE KINGDOM OF GOD

"Seek first the Kingdom of God."

This was the command of the Savior, while on the earth, teaching the children of men.

Having taken a general view of the prophecies, past and future, we shall now proceed to fulfil this command, and search out the kingdom of God. But, before we advance, I would again caution the reader not to accompany me in this research, unless he is prepared to sacrifice everything, even to his good name, and life itself, if necessary, for the truth; for if he should once get a view of the kingdom of God, he will be so delighted that he never will rest satisfied short of becoming a subject of the same. And yet it will be so unlike every other system of religion now on earth, that he will be astonished that any person, with the Bible in his hand, should ever have mistaken any of the systems of men for the kingdom of God. There are certain powers, privileges, and blessings, pertaining to the kingdom of God, which are found in no other kingdom, nor enjoyed by any other people. By these it was over distinguished from all other kingdoms and systems, insomuch that the inquiring mind, seeking the kingdom of God, and being once acquainted with these peculiarities concerning it, need never mistake it, or be at a loss to know when he has found it. But, before we proceed any further in our research, let us agree upon the meaning of the term, the Kingdom of God, or the sense in which we will use it; for some apply this term to the kingdom of glory above, and some to the individual enjoyment of their own souls, while others apply it to His organized government on the earth. Now, when We speak of the kingdom of God, we wish it to be understood that we mean His organized government on the earth.

Now, reader, we launch forth into the wide field before us in search of a kingdom. But stop, let us consider—what is a kingdom? I reply, that four things are required in order to constitute any kingdom in heaven or on earth; namely, first, a king; secondly, commissioned officers duly qualified to execute his ordinances and laws; thirdly, a code of laws by which the subjects are governed; and fourthly, subjects who are governed. Where these exist in their proper order and regular authority, there is a kingdom, but where either of these ceases to exist, there is a disorganization of the kingdom; consequently an end of it, until reorganized after the same manner as before. It this respect the kingdom of God is like all other kingdoms; wherever we find officers duly commissioned and qualified by the Lord Jesus, together with His ordinances and laws existing in purity, unmixed with any precepts or commandments of men, there the kingdom of God exists, and there His power is manifest, and His blessings are enjoyed as in days of old.

We shall now take a view of the setting up of the kingdom of God in the days of the Apostles. The first intimation of its near approach was by an angel to Zachariah, promising him a son, who should go before the King to prepare his way. The next manifestation was to Mary, and finally to Joseph, by a holy angel, promising the birth of the Messiah: while at the same time, the Holy Ghost manifested unto Simeon, in the temple, that he should not die until he had seen the Savior. Thus, all these, together with the shepherds and the wise men from the east, began to rejoice with a joy unspeakable and full of glory, while the world around them knew not the occasion of their joy. After these things, all seemed to rest in silent expectation, until John had grown to manhood, when he came bounding from the wilderness of Judea, with a proclamation strange and new, crying: "Repent ye, for the kingdom of heaven is at hand," baptizing unto repentance, telling them plainly that their King was already standing among them, on the point of setting up His kingdom. And while he yet ministered, the Messiah came, and was baptized, and sealed with the Spirit of God, which rested on Him in the form of a dove; and soon after began the same proclamation as John, saying—"Repent ye, for the kingdom of heaven is at hand." Then, after choosing twelve disciples, He sent them forth into all the cities of Judea, with the same proclamation— "The kingdom of heaven is at hand;" and after them He sent seventy, and then another seventy, with the same news, so that all might be well warned and prepared for a kingdom which was soon to be organized amongst them.

But when these things had produced the desired effect, in causing a general expectation, more especially in the hearts of His disciples, who daily expected to triumph over their persecutors, by the coronation of this glorious personage, while they themselves were hoping for a reward for all their toil and sacrifices for His sake, by being exalted to dignity near His person, what must have been their disappointment, when they saw their King taken and crucified, having been mocked, derided, ridiculed, and finally overcome, and triumphed over, both by Jew and Gentile? They would gladly have died in battle to have placed Him upon the throne; but tamely to submit without a struggle, to give up all their expectations, and sink in despair from the highest pitch of enthusiasm to the lowest degradation, was more than they could well endure. They shrank back in sorrow, and returned every man to his own net, or to their several occupations, supposing all was over; probably with reflections like these: "Is this the result of all our labors? was it for this we forsook all worldly objects, our friends, our houses and lands, suffering persecution, hunger, fatigue and disgrace? And we trust it should have been He who would have delivered Israel; but alas, they have killed Him, and all is over. For three years we have awakened a general expectation through all Judea, by telling them that the kingdom of heaven was at hand, but now our King is dead, how shall we dare to look the people in the face?"

With these reflections, each pursuing his own course, all was again turned to silence, and the voice had ceased to be heard in Judea, crying: "Repent ye, for the kingdom of heaven is at hand." Jesus slept in the arms of death; a great stone with the seal of of state, secured the tomb where he lay, while the Roman guard stood in watchful silence, to see that all was kept secure; when suddenly, from the regions of glory, a mighty angel descended, at whoso presence the soldiers fell back as dead men, while he rolled the stone from the door of the sepulchre, and the Son of God awoke from His slumbers, burst the bonds of death, and soon after appearing to Mary, He sent her to the disciples with the joyful news of His resurrection, and appointed a place to meet them. When, after seeing Him, all their sorrow was turned into joy, and all their former hopes were suddenly revived, they had no longer to cry—"The kingdom of heaven is at hand," but were to tarry at Jerusalem until the kingdom was established; and they prepared to unlock the door of the kingdom, and to adopt strangers and foreigners into it as legal citizens, by administering certain laws and ordinances, which were invariably the laws of adoption, and without which no man could ever become a citizen.

Having ascended up on high, and having been crowned with all power in heaven and on earth, He again comes to His disciples, and gives them their authority, saying unto them: "Go ye into all the world, and preach the gospel to every creature. He that believeth, and is baptized, shall be saved; but he that believeth not shall be damned. And these signs shall follow them that believe: In my name shall they cast out devils; they shall speak with new tongues; they shall take up serpents; and if they drink any deadly thing it shall not hurt them; they shall lay hands on the sick, and they shall recover." Mark, xvi, 15-18. Now I wish the reader not to pass over this commission until he understands it, because when once understood, he never need mistake the kingdom of God, but will at once discover those peculiarities which were forever to distinguish it from all other kingdoms or religious systems on earth. Lest he should misunderstand, we will analyze it, and look at each part carefully in its own proper light; first, they were to preach the Gospel, or in other words, the glad tidings of a crucified and risen Redeemer, to all the world; secondly, he that believed, and was baptized, should be saved; thirdly, he that did not believe what they preached should be damned; and fourthly, these signs should follow them that believed: first, they were to cast out devils; second, to speak with new tongues; third, to take up serpents; fourth, if they drank any deadly thing, it should not hurt them; fifth, they were to lay hands on the sick, and they should recover.

Now, it is wilful blindness, or ignorance of the English language, that has ever caused any misunderstanding here. For some tell us that those signs were only to follow the Apostles; and others, that they were only to follow believers in that age. But Christ places the preaching, believing, salvation, and the signs that were to follow, all on an equal footing; where one was limited, the other must be; where one ceased, the other did. If the language limits these signs to the Apostles, it limits faith and salvation also to them. If no others were to have these signs follow them, then no others were to believe, and no others were to be saved. Again, if the language limits these signs to the first age or ages of Christianity, then it limits salvation to the first ages of Christianity, for one is precisely as much limited as the other; and where one is in force, the other is; and where one ends, the other must stop. And as well might we say, preaching of the Gospel is no longer needed; neither faith nor salvation; these were only given at first to establish the Gospel; as to say, the signs are no longer necessary, they were only given at first to establish the Gospel. But, says the astonished reader: "Have not these signs ceased from among men?" I reply, prove that they have ceased, and it will prove that the Gospel has ceased to be preached, that men have ceased to believe and be saved, and that the world is without the kingdom of God; or else it will prove that Jesus Christ was an impostor, and His promises of no effect.

Now, having analyzed and understood this commission, let us still pursue the subject of the organization of the kingdom of God in the days of the Apostles. The Savior, having given them their authority, commands them to tarry, and not undertake their mission, until they were endowed with power from on high. But why this delay? Because no man was ever qualified, or ever will be, to preach the Gospel, and teach all things whatsoever Jesus commanded him, without the Holy Ghost; and a very different Holy Ghost, too, from the one enjoyed by men who are not inspired, for the Holy Ghost of which Jesus spake would guide into all truth, bring all things to remembrance, whatsoever He had said unto them, and show them things to come—not to mention that it would enable them to speak in all the languages of the earth. Now, a man who preaches needs that Holy Ghost very much; first, to guide into all truth, that he may know what to teach; second, to strengthen his memory, lest he might neglect to teach some of the things which were commanded him; and, third, he needs to know things to come, that he may forewarn his hearers of approaching danger, and that would constitute him a prophet. From this, the reader may see how careful Jesus was that none should preach His Gospel without the Holy Ghost. He may also learn how different the Spirit of Truth is from the spirit now abroad in the earth, deceiving the world, under the name of the Holy Ghost. If the churches of the present day have the Holy Ghost, why are they so much at a loss to understand truth? Why do they walk in so many different ways and doctrines? Why do they need whole libraries of sermons, tracts, divinities, debates, arguments, and opinions, all written by the wisdom of men, without even professing to be inspired? Well doth the Lord complain, saying: "Their fear toward me is taught by the precepts of men." But to return; the Apostles tarried at Jerusalem until endowed with power, and then they commenced to proclaim the Gospel.

Here we have discovered several things towards a kingdom: first, we have found a King, crowned at the right hand of God, to whom is committed all power in heaven and on earth; second, commissioned officers, duly appointed to administer the affairs of government; third, the laws by which they were to be governed were ALL THINGS WHATSOEVER JESUS HAD COMMANDED HIS DISCIPLES TO TEACH THEM.

And now, if we can find how men became citizens of that kingdom, I mean as to the rules of adoption, then we have found the kingdom of God in that age, and shall be very much dissatisfied with every thing in our own age, professing to be the kingdom of God, which is not according to the pattern.

It happened that there were no natural born subjects of that kingdom, for both Jew and Gentile were included in sin and unbelief; and none could be citizens without the law of adoption. All that believed on the name of the King had power to be adopted, but there was but one invariable rule or plan by which they were adopted; and all that undertook to claim citizenship, in any other way whatever, were counted thieves and robbers, and could never obtain the seal of adoption. This rule was laid down in the Savior's teaching to Nicodemus, namely: "Except a man be born of water (that is, baptized in water), and of the Spirit (that is, baptized with the Spirit), he cannot enter into the kingdom of God."

Now, to Peter were given the keys of the kingdom; therefore it was his duty to open the kingdom to Jew and also to Gentile. We will therefore carefully examine the manner in which he did adopt the Jews into the kingdom on the day of Pentecost.

Now, when the multitude came running together on the day of Pentecost, the Apostle Peter, standing up with the eleven, lifted up his voice and reasoned with them from the Scriptures, testifying of Jesus Christ, and His resurrection and ascension on high—insomuch that many became convinced of the truth, and inquired what they should do. These were not Christians, but they were people who were that moment convinced that Jesus was the Christ; and because they were convinced of this fact, they inquired—"What shall we do?" Then Peter said unto them: "Repent and be baptized, every one of you, in the name of Jesus Christ, for the remission of sins, and you shall receive the gift of the Holy Ghost: for the promise is unto you, and your children, and to all that are afar of, even as many as the Lord our God shall call." My reader, do you understand this proclamation? If you do, you will see that this Gospel is not generally preached in modern times. Let us therefore analyze and examine it, sentence by sentence. You recollect they already believed, and the next thing was for them to repent; first, faith; second, repentance; third, baptism; fourth, remission of sins; and fifth, the Holy Ghost. This was the order of the Gospel. Faith gave the power to become sons, or citizens; repentance, and baptism in His name, was the obedience through which they were adopted; and the Holy Spirit of promise was the seal of their adoption, and this they were sure to receive if they would obey.

Now, reader, where do you hear such preaching in our day? Who teaches that those who believe and repent, should be baptized, and none others? Perhaps the reader may say the Baptists do; but do they call upon men to be baptized as soon as they believe and repent? And moreover, do they promise the remission of sins, with the gift of the Holy Ghost? Recollect, now, what effect the Holy Ghost has upon people who receive it. It will guide them into all truth, strengthen the memory, and show them things to come. And Joel has said, it would cause them to dream dreams, to see visions, and to prophesy. O! my reader, where do you find a Gospel like this preached among men? Would men go mourning for weeks upon weeks, without the forgiveness of sins, or the comfort of the Holy Spirit, if Peter stood among us to tell precisely how to get such blessings? Now, what would you think of a camp meeting, where three thousand men should come forward to be prayed for, and one of the ministers should (Peter like) command them every one to repent, and be baptized for the remission of sins, promising that all who obeyed should receive the remission of sins and the gift of the Holy Ghost, which should cause them to dream dreams and prophesy; and then should arise with his brethren of the same calling, and the same hour commence baptizing, and continue until they had baptized them all; and the Holy Ghost should fall upon them, and they begin to see visions, speak in other tongues, and prophecy? Would not the news go abroad, far and wide, that a new doctrine had made its appearance, quite different from any thing now practised among men? O yes, says the reader, this, to be sure, would be something new, and very strange to all of us. Well, strange as it may seem, it is the Gospel, as preached by Peter on the day of Pentecost; and Paul declares that he preached the same Gospel that Peter did; and he has also said: "Though we, or an angel from heaven, preach any other gospel, let him be accursed." Now, the reader need no longer be astonished to see that these signs do not follow them that believe some other gospel, or doctrine, different from that preached by the Apostles.

But now let us return to the kingdom of God organized in the days of the Apostles; you discover that three thousand persons were adopted into the kingdom the first day the door was opened. These, together with the numerous additions which were afterwards made, were the subjects of this kingdom; which, being fitly framed together, grew into a holy temple in the Lord. Thus, we have cleared away the rubbish of sectarian tradition and superstition, which arose in heaps around us; and having searched carefully, we have at length discovered the kingdom of God, as it existed at its first organization in the days of the Apostles; and we have seen that it differs widely from all modern systems of religion, both in its offices, ordinances, powers, and privileges, insomuch that no man need ever mistake the one for the other.

Having made this discovery, we shall proceed to examine the progress of the kingdom among Jew and Gentile; and what were its fruits, gifts, and blessings as enjoyed by its citizens.

Soon after the organization of the kingdom of God at Jerusalem, Philip came to Samaria, and there preached the Gospel: and when they believed Philip, they were baptized, both men and women, and had great joy. And afterwards, Peter and John came from Jerusalem, and prayed, and laid their hands on them, and they received the Holy Ghost. Mark here, they first believed, and then were baptized, having great joy, and yet had not received the Holy Ghost. But that was afterwards given, by the laying on of hands and prayer, in the name of Jesus. O how different from the systems of men!

Witness Paul's conversion while on his journey to Damascus: the Lord Jesus appeared to him in the way; but instead of telling him his sins were forgiven, and pouring the Holy Ghost upon him, He sent him to Damascus, telling him that it should there be told him what he should do. And coming to Damascus, Ananias being sent, commanded him not to tarry, but to "arise and be baptized, and wash away his sins, calling on the name of the Lord;" then he arose and was baptized, and was even filled with the Holy Ghost, and straightway preached that Jesus was the Christ.

Again, witness Peter going to Cornelius, a Gentile of great piety, whose prayers were heard, and whose alms were remembered, and who had even attained to the ministering of an angel; yet with all his piety, and the Holy Ghost poured out upon him and his friends, before they were baptized, they must be baptized, or they could not be saved. Why? Because the Lord had commanded the Apostles to preach to every creature, and every creature who would not believe and be baptized, should be damned, without one exception. Witness the words of the angel to Cornelius: "He (Peter) shall tell thee words whereby thou and all thy house shall be saved." Now, query, could Cornelius have been saved without obeying the words of Peter? If so, the angel's errand was in vain.

Now, perhaps a minister, who should find a man as good as Cornelius was, would say to him: "Go on, brother, you can be saved, you have experienced religion, you may indeed be baptized to answer a good conscience, if you feel it your duty; or, if not, it is no matter, a new heart is all that is really necessary to salvation," etc.; as much as to say, that the commandments of Jesus are not absolutely necessary to salvation; a man may call him Lord, Lord, and be saved, just as well as by keeping His commandments. Oh vain and foolish doctrine! Oh ye children of men, how have you perverted the Gospel! In vain do ye call Him Lord, Lord, and do not obey His commandments.

Next, we call to mind the jailor and his household, who were baptized the same hour they believed, without waiting for the day; and Lydia and her household, who attended to the ordinance the first sermon they heard on the subject. Also Philip and the eunuch, who stopped the chariot at the first water they came to, in order to attend to the ordinance, although the eunuch had heard of Jesus, for the first time, only a few minutes before. Now, I gather from all those examples of ancient days, and from the precepts laid down in them, that baptism was the initiating ordinance, by which all those who believed and repented were received and adopted into the church or kingdom of God, so as to be entitled to the remission of sins, and the blessing of the Holy Ghost; indeed, it was the ordinance through which they became sons and daughters; and because they were sons, the Lord shed forth the Spirit of His Son into their hearts, crying, Abba, Father. It is true, the Lord poured out the Holy Ghost upon Cornelius and his friends, before they were baptized; but it seemed necessary, in order to convince the believing Jews that the Gentiles also had part in this salvation. And I believe this is the only instance, in the whole record, of the people receiving the Holy Ghost without first obeying the laws of adoption. But mark! Obeying the laws of adoption would not constitute a man an heir of the kingdom, a citizen entitled to the blessings and gifts of the Spirit, unless those laws and ordinances were administered by one who had proper authority, and was duly commissioned from the King; and a commission given to one individual could never authorize another to act in his stead. This is one of the most important points to be understood, as it brings to the test every minister in Christendom; and questions the organization of every church on earth, and all that have existed since direct inspiration ceased.

Now, in order to come at this subject in plainness, let us examine the constitution of earthly governments in regard to the authority and laws of adoption. We will say, for instance, the President of the United States writes a commission to A. B., duly authorizing him to act in some office in the government, and, during his administration, two gentlemen from Europe come to reside in this country, and, being strangers and foreigners wishing to become citizens, they go before A. B., and he administers the oath of allegiance in due form, and certifies the same, and this constitutes them legal citizens, entitled to all the privileges of those who are citizens or subjects by birth. After these things, A. B. is taken away by death, and C. D., in looking over his papers, happens to find the commission given to A. B., and, applying it to his own use, assumes the vacant office; meantime, two foreigners arrive, and apply for citizenship, and being informed by persons ignorant of the affairs of government, that C. D. could administer the laws of adoption, they submit to be administered unto by C. D., without once examining his authority; C. D. certifies of their citizenship, and they suppose they have been legally adopted, the same as the others, and are entitled to all the privileges of citizenship. But by and by, their citizenship is called in question, and they produce the certificate of C. D.; the President inquires— "Who is C. D.? I never gave him a commission to act in any office, I know him not, and you are strangers and foreigners to the commonwealth, until you go before the legally appointed successor of A. B., or some other of like authority, who has a commission from the President direct in his own name." In the meantime, C. D. is taken and punished according to law, for practising imposition, and usurping authority which was never conferred upon him.

And so it is with the kingdom of God. The Lord authorized the Apostles and others by direct revelation, and by the spirit of prophecy, to preach and baptize, and build up His church and kingdom; but after a while they died, and a long time passed away, and men, reading over their commission, where it says to the eleven Apostles—"Go ye into all the world and preach the Gospel to every creature," etc., have had the presumption to apply these sayings as their authority, and without any other commission, have gone forth professing to preach the Gospel, and baptize, and build up the church and kingdom of God; but those whom they baptize never receive the same blessings and gifts which characterized a saint or citizen of the kingdom in the days of the Apostles. Why? Because they are yet foreigners and strangers, for the commission given to the Apostles never commissioned any other man to act in their stead. This was a prerogative the Lord reserved unto himself. No man has a right to take this ministry upon himself, but he that is called by revelation, and duly qualified to act in his calling by the Holy Ghost.

But the reader inquires with astonishment, "What! are none of all the ministers of the present day called to the ministry, and legally commissioned?" Well, my reader, I will tell you how you may ascertain from their own mouths, and that will be far better than an answer from me; go to the clergy, and ask them if God has given them any direct revelation since the New Testament was finished; inquire of them whether the gift of prophecy ceased with the early age of the church; and, in short, ask them if revelations, prophets, the ministering of angels, etc., are needed or expected in these days, or whether they believe that these things are done away, no more to return to the earth; and their answer will be that the Bible contains sufficient, and that since the canon of Scripture was filled, revelation, the spirit of prophecy and the ministering of angels have ceased, because no longer needed. In short, they will denounce every man as an impostor who pretends to any such thing. And when you have obtained this answer, ask them how they themselves were called and commissioned to preach the Gospel, and they will be at a loss to answer you, and will finally tell you that the Bible commissioned them, saying — "Go ye into all the world," etc. Thus, you see, all who have no direct personal revelation from the King of heaven, either by angels, the voice of God, or the spirit of prophecy, are acting under authority which was given to others, who are dead, and their commission stolen, and their authority usurped; and the King will say — "Peter I know, and Paul I know, I commissioned them, but who are you? I know you not, I never spoke to you in my life; indeed you believed it was not necessary for me to speak in your day. Therefore you never sought in faith for any revelation, and I never gave you any; and even when I spake to others, you mocked them, and called them impostors, and persecuted them, because they testified of the things I had said unto them, therefore depart from me, ye cursed, into everlasting fire, prepared for the devil and his angels: for I was an hungered, and ye fed me not; I was naked, and ye clothed me not; I was a stranger, and ye took me not in; sick and in prison and ye visited me not." "Ah! Lord, when did we fail in any of these things?" "Inasmuch as you have not done it unto the least of these my brethren (taking them for impostors, because they testified of the things which I had revealed unto them), ye have not done it unto me." But to return: having examined the kingdom of God as to its offices and ordinances, and having discovered the only means of adoption into it, let us examine more fully what are the blessings, privileges, and enjoyments of its citizens. You have already seen that they were to cast out devils, speak with new tongues, heal the sick by the laying on of hands in the name of Jesus, as well as to see visions, dream dreams, prophesy, etc.

But let us look at the kingdom in its organized state, and see whether these promises were verified to Jew and Gentile, wherever the kingdom of God was found in all ages of the world.

Paul writing, first, "To the church of God at Corinth;" second, "To them that are sanctified in Christ Jesus;" third, "To them who are called to be saints;" and fourth, "To all that in every place call on the name of Jesus Christ our Lord," says to them all, in 1 Corinthians, xii, 1: "Now, concerning spiritual gifts, brethren, I would not have you ignorant." And then, continuing his instructions, a few verses further on, he says: "But the manifestation of the Spirit is given to every man to profit withal; for to one is given, by the Spirit, the word of wisdom; to another the word of knowledge by the same Spirit; to another faith by the same Spirit; to another, the gifts of healing by the same Spirit; to another, the working of miracles; to another, prophecy; to another, discerning of spirits; to another, divers kinds of tongues; to another, the interpretation of tongues; but all these worketh that one and the self-same Spirit, dividing to every man severally as He (Christ) will. For as the body is one, and hath many members, and all the members of that one body, being many, are one body; so also is Christ. For by one Spirit are we all baptized into one body, whether we be Jews or Gentiles, whether we be bond or free; and have been all made to drink into one Spirit. For the body is not one member, but many. If the foot shall say, because I am not the hand, I am not of the body; is it therefore not of the body? And if the ear shall say, because I am not the eye, I am not of the body; is it therefore not of the body? If the whole body were an eye, where were the hearing? If the whole were hearing, where were the smelling? But now hath Got set the members, everyone of them in the body, as it hath pleased Him. And if they were all one member, where were the body?" I reply, it would not exist. "But now are they many members, yet but one body. And the eye cannot say unto the hand, I have no need of thee; nor again, the head to the feet, I have no need of you. Nay, much more those members of the body which seem to be more feeble, are necessary; and those members of the body which we think to be less honorable, upon these we bestow more abundant honor: and our uncomely parts have more abundant comeliness. For our comely parts have no need: but God hath tempered the body together, having given more abundant honor to that part which lacked: that there should be no schism in the body; but that the members should have the same care for one another. And whether one member suffer, all the members suffer with it; or one member be honored, all the members rejoice with it. Now, ye are the body of Christ, and members in particular. And God hath set some in the church, first, apostles; secondarily, prophets; thirdly, teachers; after that, miracles, then gifts of healings, helps, governments, diversities of tongues. Are all apostles? are all prophets? are all teachers? are all workers of miracles? Have all the gifts of healing? do all speak with tongues? do all interpret? But covet earnestly the best gifts: and yet shew I unto you a more excellent way." From the thirteenth verse of the above chapter, we learn that the Apostle is still speaking to the whole church in all ages, whether Jew or Gentile, bond or free, even all who should ever compose the body of Christ, and showing that Christ's body consisted of many members, baptized by one spirit into one body, possessing all these different gifts, some one gift, and some another: and then expressly says, that one member possessing one gift, should not say to another member possessing another gift, we have no need of thee.

And having shown that it required apostles, prophets, evangelists, pastors, and teachers; together with the gifts of prophecy, miracles, healing, and all other gifts, to compose the church, or body of Christ, in any age, whether Jew or Gentile, bond or free; and having utterly forbidden any of the members ever to say, of any of these gifts: "We have no need of thee," He declares the body never could be perfected without all of them, and that if they were done away, there would be no body, that is, no church of Christ in existence. Having shown all these things clearly, he exhorts them to covet earnestly the best gifts. And in the thirteenth chapter, exhorts them to faith, hope, and charity, without which all these gifts would avail them nothing: and in the fourteenth chapter repeats the exhortation: "Follow after charity, and desire spiritual gifts, but rather that ye may prophesy." Again, in Ephesians, i, 17, Paul prays that the Lord would give unto the church the Spirit of WISDOM and of REVELATION, in the KNOWLEDGE of God. Again, in Ephesians, iv, he tells them there is one body and one Lord, one Spirit, one faith, and one baptism; and that Christ ascended up on high, led captivity captive, and gave gifts to men. And He gave some apostles; and some, prophets; and some, evangelists; and some, pastors and teachers. And if the reader inquire what these gifts or offices were for, let him read the twelfth verse: "For the perfecting of the saints, for the work of the ministry, for the edifying of the body of Christ." And if he inquire how long these were to continue, the thirteenth verse says: "Till we all come in the unity of the faith, and of the knowledge of the Son of God, unto a perfect man, unto the measure of the stature of the fulness of Christ." And if he still inquire what further object Christ had in giving these gifts, let him read the fourteenth verse: "That we henceforth be no more children, tossed to and fro, and carried about with every wind of doctrine, by the sleight of men, and cunning craftiness, whereby they lie in wait to deceive."

Now, without these gifts and offices, first, the saints cannot be perfected; second, the work of the ministry cannot proceed; third, the body of Christ cannot be edified; and fourth, there is nothing to prevent them from being carried about with every wind of doctrine. Now, I boldly declare that the cause of all the division, confusion, jars, discord, and animosities; and the fruitful source of so many faiths, lords, baptisms, and spirits; and of the understanding being darkened; and of men being alienated from the life of God, through the ignorance that is in them, because of the blindness of their hearts, is, because they have neither apostles, prophets, nor gifts, inspired from on high, to whom they give heed; for, if they had such gifts, and would give heed unto them, they would be built up in one body, in the pure doctrine of Christ, having one Lord, one faith, one baptism, and one hope of their calling; yea, they would be edified, built up unto Christ in all things, in whom the whole body, fitly joined together, would grow into an holy temple in the Lord.

But so long as the cunning craftiness of men can persuade them that they have no need of these things, so long they can toss them about with every wind of doctrine, just as they please.

Now, reader, I have done our examination of the kingdom of God, as it existed in the Apostles' days; and we cannot look at it in any other age, until renewed again in the last days, for it never did, nor never will exist, without apostles and prophets, and all the other gifts of the Spirit.

Were we to take a view of the churches, from the days that inspiration ceased until now, we should see nothing like the kingdom which we have been viewing with such admiration and delight. But instead of apostles and prophets, we should see false teachers, whom men had heaped to themselves; and instead of the gifts of the Spirit, we should see the wisdom of men; and instead of the Holy Ghost, many false spirits; instead of the ordinances of God, commandments of men; instead of knowledge, opinion; guess work, instead of revelation; division, instead of union; doubt, instead of faith; despair, instead of hope; hatred, instead of charity; a physician, instead of the laying on of hands for the healing of the sick; fables, instead of truth, evil for good, good for evil; darkness for light, light for darkness, and in a word, anti-Christ instead of Christ; the powers of earth having made war with the saints, and overcome them, until the words of God should be fulfilled.

O my God, shut up the vision! for my heart sickens while I gaze; and let the day hasten on when the earth shall be cleansed by fire from such awful pollutions; but first, let Thy promise be fulfilled, which Thou didst make by the mouth of Thy servant John, that Thou wouldst call Thy people out of her, saying: "Come out of her, my people, that ye be not partakers of her sins, and that ye receive not of her plagues;" and then, O Lord, when Thou hast called Thy people out from the midst of her, by the fishers and hunters whom Thou hast promised to send in the last days to gather Israel; yea, when Thine everlasting covenant has been renewed, and Thy people established thereby; then let her plagues come in one day, death, mourning, and famine; let her be burned with fire; that the holy Apostles and Prophets, and all that fear Thy name, small and great, may rejoice, because Thou hast avenged the blood of Thy saints upon her. I ask these things in the name of Jesus Christ. Amen.

CHAPTER IV

THE BOOK OF MORMON – ORIGIN OF THE AMERICAN INDIANS, ETC

Ye gloomy scenes, far hence, intrude no more!

Sublimer themes invite the muse to soar

In loftier strains, while scenes both strange and new

Burst on the sight, and open to the view.

Lo! from the opening heavens, in bright array

An angel comes – to earth he bends his way:

Reveals to man, in power, as at the first,

The fulness of the Gospel long since lost.

See earth, obedient, from its bosom yield

The sacred truth it faithfully concealed.

The wise, confounded, startle at the sight,

The proud and haughty tremble with affright.

The hireling priests against the truth engage,

While hell beneath stands trembling, filled with rage;

False are their hopes, and all their struggles vain;

Their craft must fall, and with it all their gain;

The deaf must hear, the meek their joy increase;

The poor be glad, and their oppression cease.

While darkness covered the earth, and gross darkness the people, every man walking in his own way, and looking for gain from his quarter, the Lord having for a long time held His peace, and the people having fondly flattered themselves that the voice of inspiration would never again sound in the ears of mortals, to disturb or molest them in their sinful career; while a few were looking for the consolation of Israel, and crying to God for the ushering in of that long-expected day, when an angel should fly through the midst of heaven, having the everlasting Gospel to preach unto them that dwell on the earth— suddenly, a voice is heard from the wilderness, a cry salutes the ears of mortals, a testimony is heard among them, piercing to the inmost recesses of their hearts, when all at once the heathen begin to rage, and the people to imagine a vain thing; the clergy lift a warning voice, crying impostor, false prophets, beware of delusion, etc.; while the professor of religion, the drunkard, the swearer, the learned, and the ignorant soon catch the sound and reiterate it again and again. Thus it re-echoes from one end of our country to the other, for a long time, and if any one should be so fortunate as to retain his sober senses, and should candidly inquire, "What is the matter?" the reply is: "We hardly know anything about it, but suffice it to say, some fellows have made their appearance, Paul like, who testify something about the ministering of angels, or some revelation or inspiration, just as though the religion of ancient days, and the faith once delivered to the saints, were returning to the earth in this enlightened age; so that not only this our craft is in danger, but our modern systems of religion, built upon the wisdom and learning of men, without direct inspiration, are like to be spoken against, and their great magnificence despised, though worshiped by all the world." And then all again cry with a loud voice, saying: "Great is the wisdom of man; great are the systems of modern divinity; great is the wisdom of uninspired priests, who come unto us with excellency of speech, and with man's wisdom, determined to know nothing among us save opinions and creeds of their own; and their speech, and their preaching, are with enticing words of man's wisdom, not in demonstration of the Spirit, and of power, for that is done away, that our faith should not stand in the power of God, but in the wisdom of man."

In the midst of the noise and clamor, and prejudice of an opposing world, it is difficult to get the people to understand the facts of the case, in relation to one of the most important subjects ever presented to the consideration of mankind.

The Book of Mormon has perhaps been less understood, and more misrepresented, by the world at large, than any other publication which has ever appeared.

America and England have, as it were, been flooded with publications against the said book; and many of them written by those who had never seen the book, or by those who had only read a page or two in it, or slightly looked it through with a biased mind, and a determination to find fault. By some of these it has been represented as a romance; by others, as a new Bible, calculated to displace the Bible, or do away with it. Some have pronounced it a "silly mess of stuff," not worth the perusal; and others, the most ingenious literary work ever put together. Some have found fault with it for being so much like the Bible, and agreeing with it; and others have condemned it for not being sufficiently like the Bible, and for disagreeing with it. Some have denounced it as notoriously corrupt, immoral, and blasphemous in its principles; and others have condemned it for being so exceedingly pure and moral in its principles, as to be just calculated to deceive. One clergyman, in particular, in a tract of sixty pages on this book, condemns it for being "a strange mixture of faith and works, of themercy of God and the obedience of the creature." Some literary persons have pronounced it as altogether ancient in its style, language, and subjects, and as bearing great internal evidence of its own antiquity; while others have condemned it, as bearing every mark of being a modern production. Some have said that there were no definite predictions of the future contained in it, by the fulfilment or failure of which its prophetic merits might be tested; and others have quoted largely from its most plain and pointed predictions, which relate to circumstances about to be fulfilled, and have condemned it on account of its plainness.

In the midst of all these jarring statements, it now becomes our duty to show, as far as possible, what the Book of Mormon really is.

When the Lord confounded the languages at Babel, he led forth a colony from thence to the Western Continent, which is now called America. This colony, after crossing the ocean in eight vessels, and landing in that country, became, in process of time, a great nation—they inhabited America for some fifteen hundred years. They were at length destroyed for their wickedness, about six hundred years before Christ. A prophet by the name of Ether wrote their history, and an account of their destruction.

Ether lived to witness their entire destruction, and deposited his record where it was afterwards found by a colony of Israelites, who came from Jerusalem six hundred years before Christ, and re-peopled America. This last colony were the descendants of the tribe of Joseph; they grew and multiplied, and finally gave rise to two mighty nations. One of these nations was called Nephites—one Nephi being their founder; the other was called Lamanites, after a leader of the name Laman.

The Lamanites became a dark and benighted people, of whom the American Indians are still a remnant. The Nephites were an enlightened and civilized people, they were a people highly favored of the Lord, they had visions, angels, and the gift of prophecy among them from age to age; and finally, they were blessed with a personal appearance of Jesus Christ after his resurrection, from whose mouth they received the doctrine of the Gospel, and a knowledge of the future down through all succeeding ages. But after all the blessings and privileges conferred upon them, they fell into great wickedness in the third and fourth centuries of the Christian era, and finally were destroyed by the hands of the Lamanites. This destruction took place about four hundred years after Christ.

Mormon lived in that age of the world, and was a Nephite, and a Prophet of the Lord. He, by the commandment of the Lord, made an abridgment of the sacred records, which contained the history of his forefathers, and the Prophecies and Gospel which had been revealed among them; to which he added a sketch of the history of his own time, and the destruction of his nation. Previous to his death, the abridged records fell into the hands of his son Moroni, who continued them down to A. D. 420; at which time he deposited them carefully in the earth, on a hill which was then called Cumorah, but is situated in Ontario County, township of Manchester, and State of New York, North America. This he did in order to preserve them from the Lamanites, who overran the country, and sought to destroy them and all the records pertaining to the Nephites. This record lay concealed, or sealed up, from A. D. 420 to September 22, 1827, at which time it was found by Mr. Joseph Smith, jun., he being directed thither by an angel of the Lord.

The following account of the discovery and translation of this record is extracted from a tract by Elder Orson Pratt, published at Edinburgh, in 1840, entitled, "Remarkable Visions," etc., to which our readers are referred for further particulars: —

"'How far below the surface these records were placed by Moroni, I am unable to say; but from the fact that they had been some fourteen hundred years buried, and that, too, on the side of a hill so steep, one is ready to conclude that they were some feet below, as the earth would naturally wear, more or less, in that length of time; but they being placed toward the top of the hill, the ground would not remove as much as at two-thirds, perhaps. Another circumstance would prevent a wearing of the earth; in all probability, as soon as timber had time to grow, the hill was covered, after the Nephites were destroyed, and the roots of the same would hold the surface: however, on this point, I shall leave every man to draw his own conclusion, and form his own speculation.' But suffice it to say, 'a hole of sufficient depth was dug; at the bottom of this was laid a stone of suitable size, the upper surface being smooth; at each edge was placed a large quantity of cement, and into this cement, at the four edges of this stone, were placed erect four others; their bottom edges resting in the cement, at the outer edges of the first stone. The four last named, when placed erect, formed a box; the corners, or where the edges of the four came in contact, were also cemented so firmly, that the moisture from without was prevented from entering. It is to be observed, also, that the inner surface of the four erect or side stones was smooth. This box was sufficiently large to admit a breastplate, such as was used by the ancients to defend the chest, etc., from the arrows and weapons of their enemy.

From the bottom of the box, or from the breastplate, arose three small pillars, composed of the same description of cement used on the edges; and upon these three pillars was placed the record. This box containing the record was covered with another stone, the bottom surface being flat, and the upper crowning.' When it was first visited by Mr. Smith, on the morning of the twenty-second of September, 1823, 'a part of the crowning stone was visible above the surface, while the edges were concealed by the soil and grass. From which circumstance, it may be seen, that however deep this box might have been placed by Moroni at first, the time had been sufficient to wear the earth, so that it was easily discovered, when once directed, and yet not enough to make a perceivable difference to the passer by. After arriving at the repository, a little exertion in removing the soil from the edges of the top of the box, and a light pry, brought to his natural vision its contents.'

"While viewing and contemplating this sacred treasure with wonder and astonishment, behold! the angel of the Lord, who had previously visited him, again stood in his presence, and his soul was again enlightened as it was the evening before, and he was filled with the Holy Spirit, and the heavens were opened, and the glory of the Lord shone round about and rested upon him. 'While he thus stood, gazing and admiring, the angel said, Look!' And as he thus spake, he beheld the Prince of Darkness, surrounded by his innumerable train of associates. All this passed before him, and the heavenly messenger said: 'All this is shown, the good and the evil, the holy and impure, the glory of God, and the power of darkness, that you may know hereafter, the two powers, and never be influenced or overcome by that wicked one. Behold, whatever entices and leads to good, and to do good, is of God, and whatever does not, is of that wicked one. It is he that fills the hearts of men with evil to walk in darkness, and blaspheme God; and you may learn from henceforth, that his ways are to destruction; but the way of holiness is peace and rest. You now see why you could not obtain this record, that the commandment was strict, and that if ever these sacred things are obtained, they must be by prayer and faithfulness in obeying the Lord. They are not deposited here for the sake of accumulating gain and wealth, for the glory of this world; they were sealed by the prayer of faith, and because of the knowledge which they contain, they are of no worth among the children of men, only for their knowledge. On them is contained the fulness of the Gospel of Jesus Christ, as it was given to His people on this land; and when it shall be brought forth by the power of God, it shall be carried to the Gentiles, of whom many will receive it, and after, will the seed of Israel be brought into the fold of their Redeemer by obeying it also. Those who kept the commandments of the Lord on this land, desired this at His hand, and through the prayer of faith obtained the promise, that if their descendants should transgress and fall away, a record might be kept, and in the last days, come to their children. These things are sacred, and must be kept so, for the promise of the Lord concerning them must be fulfilled. No man can obtain them if his heart is impure, because they contain that which is sacred. By them will the Lord work a great and marvelous work; the wisdom of the wise shall become as naught, and the understanding of the prudent shall be hid, and because the power of God shall be displayed, those who profess to know the truth, but walk in deceit, shall tremble with anger; but with signs and with wonders, with gifts and with healings, with the manifestations of the power of God, and with the Holy Ghost, shall the hearts of the faithful be comforted. You have now beheld the power of God manifested, and the power of Satan; you see that there is nothing that is desirable in the works of darkness; that they cannot bring happiness; that those who are overcome therewith are miserable; while, on the other hand, the righteous are blessed with a place in the kingdom of God, where joy unspeakable surrounds them; there they rest beyond the power of the enemy of truth, where no evil can disturb them: the glory of God crowns them, and they continually feast upon His goodness, and enjoy His smiles. Behold, notwithstanding you have seen this great display of power, by which you may ever be able to detect the evil one, yet I give unto you another sign, and when it comes to pass, then know that the Lord is God, and that He will fulfil His purposes, and that the knowledge which this record contains, will go to every nation, and kindred, and tongue, and people under the whole heaven. This is the sign: when these things begin to be known, that is, when it is known that the Lord has shown you these things, the workers of iniquity will seek your overthrow; they will circulate falsehoods to destroy your reputation; and also will seek to take your life! but remember this, if you are faithful, and shall hereafter continue to keep the commandments of the Lord, you shall be preserved to bring these things forth; for in due time He will again give you a commandment to come and take them. When they are interpreted, the Lord will give the Holy Priesthood to some, and they shall begin to proclaim this Gospel and baptize by water, and after that, they shall have power to give the Holy Ghost by the laying on of their hands. Then will persecution rage more and more; for the iniquities of men shall be revealed, and those who are not built upon the Rock will seek to overthrow this Church; but it will increase the more opposed, and spread farther and farther, increasing in knowledge, till they shall be sanctified, and receive an inheritance where the glory of God will rest upon them; and when this takes place, and all things are prepared, the ten tribes of Israel will be revealed in the north country, whither they have been for a long season; and when this is fulfilled, will be brought to pass that saying of the Prophet, 'And the Redeemer shall come to Zion, and unto them that turn from transgression in Jacob, saith the Lord.' But, notwithstanding the workers of iniquity shall seek your destruction, the arm of the Lord will be extended, and you will be borne off conqueror, if you keep all His commandments. Your name shall be known among the nations, for the work which the Lord will perform by your hands shall cause the righteous to rejoice and the wicked to rage; with the one it shall be had in honor, and with the other in reproach; yet, with these it shall be a terror, because of the great and marvelous work which shall follow the coming forth of this fulness of the Gospel. Now, go thy way, remembering what the Lord has done for thee, and be diligent in keeping His commandments, and He will deliver thee from temptations, and all the arts and devices of the wicked one. Forget not to pray, that thy mind may become strong, that when he shall manifest unto thee, thou mayest have power to escape the evil, and obtain these precious things."

We here remark, that the above quotation is an extract from a letter written by Elder Oliver Cowdery, which was published in one of the numbers of the "Latter-day Saints' Messenger and Advocate."

Although many more instructions were given by the mouth of the angel to Mr. Smith, which we do not write in this book, yet the most important items are contained in the foregoing relation. During the period of the four following years, he frequently received instruction from the mouth of the heavenly messenger, and on the morning of the twenty-second of September, A. D. 1827, the angel of the Lord delivered the records into his hands.

These records were engraved on plates which had the appearance of gold. Each plate was not far from seven inches in width by eight inches in length, being not quite as thick as common tin. They were filled on both sides with engravings, in Egyptian characters, and bound together in a volume, as the leaves of a book, and fastened at one edge with three rings running through the whole. This volume was something near six inches in thickness, a part of which was sealed. The characters of letters upon the unsealed part were small, and beautifully engraved. The whole book exhibited many marks of antiquity in its construction, as well as much skill in the art of engraving. With the records was found a curious instrument, called by the ancients the Urim and Thummim, which consisted of two transparent stones, clear as crystal, set in the two rims of a bow. This was in use in ancient times by persons called Seers. It was an instrument by the use of which they received revelation of things distant, or of things past or future.

In the mean time the inhabitants of that vicinity, having been informed that Mr. Smith had seen heavenly visions, and that he had discovered sacred records, began to ridicule and mock at those things. And after having obtained those sacred things, while proceeding home through the wilderness and fields, he was waylaid by two ruffians, who had secreted themselves for the purpose of robbing him of the records. One of them struck him with a club before he perceived them; but being a strong man, and large in stature, with great exertion he cleared himself from them, and ran towards home, being closely pursued until he came near his father's house, when his pursuers, for fear of being detected, turned and fled the other way.

Soon the news of his discoveries spread abroad throughout all those parts. False reports, misrepresentations, and base slanders flew as if upon the wings of the wind in every direction. The house was frequently beset by mobs and evil designing persons. Several times he was shot at, and very narrowly escaped. Every device was used to get the plates away from him. And being continually in danger of his life, from a gang of abandoned wretches, he at length concluded to leave the place, and go to Pennsylvania; and accordingly packed up his goods, putting the plates into a barrel of beans, and proceeded upon his journey. He had not gone far, before he was overtaken by an officer with a search warrant, who flattered himself with the idea that he should surely obtain the plates; after searching very diligently, ho was sadly disappointed at not finding them. Mr. Smith then drove on; but before he got to his journey's end, he was again overtaken by an officer on the same business, and after ransacking the wagon very carefully, he went his way, as much chagrined as the first at not being able to discover the object of his research. Without any further molestation, he pursued his journey until he came into the northern part of Pennsylvania, near the Susquehanna River, in which part his father-in-law resided.

Having provided himself with a home, ho commenced translating the record, by the gift and power of God, through the means of the Urim and Thummim; and being a poor writer, he was under the necessity of employing a scribe, to write the translation as it tame from his mouth.

In the meantime, a few of the original characters were accurately transcribed and translated by Mr. Smith, which, with the translation, were taken by a gentleman named Martin Harris to the city of New York, where they were presented to a learned gentleman named Anthon, who professed to be extensively acquainted with many languages, both ancient and modern. He examined them, but was unable to decipher them correctly; but he presumed, that if the original records could be brought, he could assist in translating them.

But to return. Mr. Smith continued the work of translation, as his pecuniary circumstances would permit, until he had finished the unsealed part of the records. The part translated is entitled the "Book of Mormon," which contains nearly as much reading as the Old Testament.

"Well," says the objector, "if it were not for the marvellous, the book would be considered one of the greatest discoveries the world ever witnessed. If you had been ploughing, or digging a well or cellar and accidentally dug up a record containing some account of the ancient history of the American continent, and of its original inhabitants, together with the origin of the Indian tribes who now inhabit it; had this record had nothing to do with God, or angels, or inspiration, it would have been hailed by all the learned of America and Europe, as one of the greatest and most important discoveries of modern times, unfolding a mystery which had, until then, bid defiance to all the researches of the learned world. Every newspaper would have been filled with the glad tidings, while its contents would have poured upon the world a flood of light, on subjects before concealed in the labyrinth of uncertainty and doubt. But who can stoop, and so humble himself as to receive anything, in this enlightened age, renowned for its religion and learning, from the ministering of angels, and from inspiration? This is too much: away with such things, it comes in contact with the wisdom and popularity of the day." To this I reply, The Lord knew that before He revealed it; this was one principal object He had in view; it is just the manner of His dealing with the children of men; He always takes a different course from the one marked out for Him by the wisdom of the world, in order to "confound the wise, and bring to naught the understanding of the prudent;" He chooses men of low degree, even the simple and the unlearned, and those who are despised, to do His work and to bring about His purposes, that no flesh shall glory in His presence. O ye wise, and ye learned, who despise the wisdom that comes from above! Know ye not, that it was impossible for the world by wisdom to find out God? Know ye not that all your wisdom is foolishness with God? Know ye not that ye must become as a little child, and be willing to learn wisdom, from the least of His servants, or you will perish in your ignorance?

But what are the evidences which we gather from Scripture, concerning the coming forth of this glorious work? We shall attempt to prove: first, that America is a land promised to the seed of Joseph; second, that the Lord would reveal to them His truth as well as to the Jews; and third, that their record should come forth, and unite its testimony, with the record of the Jews, in time for the restoration of Israel, in the last days.

First, Genesis, xlviii, Jacob, while blessing the two sons of Joseph, says: "Let them grow into a multitude in the midst of the earth." In the same blessing, it is said of Ephraim, "His seed shall become a multitude of nations." Now put the sense of these sayings together, and it makes Ephraim a multitude of nations in the midst of the earth. In Genesis, xlix, it is prophesied concerning Joseph, while Jacob was blessing him, that he should be "a fruitful bough by a well, whose branches run over the wall: the archers have sorely grieved him, and shot at him, and hated him, but his bow abode in strength." Again, he further says: "The blessings of thy father have prevailed above the blessings of my progenitors, unto the utmost bound of the everlasting hills; they shall be on the head of Joseph, and on the crown of the head of him that was separate from his brethren." Now I ask, Who were Jacob's progenitors, and what was the blessing conferred upon him? Abraham and Isaac were his progenitors, and the land of Canaan was the blessing they conferred upon him, or that God promised them he should possess. Recollect that Jacob confers on Joseph a much greater land than that of Canaan; even greater than his fathers had conferred upon him, for Joseph's blessing was to extend to the uttermost bound of the everlasting hills. Now, reader, stand in Egypt, where Jacob then stood, and measure to the utmost bound of the everlasting hills, and you will land somewhere in the central part of America. Again, one of the Prophets says, in speaking of Ephraim: "When the Lord shall roar, the children of Ephraim shall tremble from the west." Now let us sum up these sayings, and what have we gained? First, that Ephraim was to grow into a multitude of nations in the midst of the earth; second, Joseph was to be greatly blessed in a large inheritance, as far off as America; third, this was to be on the west of Egypt or Jerusalem.

Now let the world search from pole to pole, and they will not find a multitude of nations in the midst of the earth, who can possibly have sprung from Ephraim, unless they find them in America; for the midst of all other parts of the earth is inhabited by mixed races, who have sprung from various sources; while here an almost boundless country was secluded from the rest of the world, and inhabited by a race of men, evidently of the same origin, although as evidently divided into many nations. Now, the Scriptures cannot be broken; therefore, these Scriptures must apply to America, for the plainest of reasons: they can apply to no other place.

Now, secondly, we are to prove that God revealed himself to the seed of Joseph or Ephraim—their location we have already proved—dwelling in America. For this, we quote Hosea, viii, 12; speaking of Ephraim, he says by the spirit of prophecy: "I have written to him the great things of my law, but they were counted as a strange thing." This is proof positive and needs no comment, that the great truths of Heaven were revealed unto Ephraim, and were counted as a strange thing.

Third: Were these writings to come forth just previously to the gathering of Israel? Answer: They were, according to Ezekiel, thirty-seventh chapter, where God commanded him to "Take one stick, and write upon it For Judah, and the children of Israel his companions; then take another stick, and write upon it For Joseph, the stick of Ephraim, and for all the house of Israel his companions; and join them one to another, into one stick, and they shall become one in thine hand. And when the children of thy people shall speak unto thee, saying, Wilt not thou show us what thou meanest by these? say unto them, Thus saith the Lord God, Behold, I will take the stick of Joseph, which is in the hand of Ephraim, and the tribes of Israel his fellows, and will put them with him, even with the stick of Judah, and make them one stick, and they shall be one in mine hand; and the sticks whereon thou writest shall be in thine hand before their eyes. And say unto them, Thus saith the Lord God, Behold, I will take the children of Israel from among the heathen, whither they be gone, and will gather them on every side, and bring them into their own land; and I will make them one nation in the land upon the mountains of Israel; and one king shall be king to them all: and they shall be no more two nations, neither shall they be divided into two kingdoms any more at all."

Now, nothing can be more plain than the above prophecy; there are presented two writings, the one to Ephraim, the other to Judah; that of Ephraim is to be brought forth by the Lord, and put with that of Judah, and they are to become one in their testimony, and grow together in this manner, in order to bring about the gathering of Israel. The eighty-fifth Psalm is very plain on the subject: speaking of the restoration of Israel to their own land, it says, "Mercy and Truth are met together; Righteousness and peace have kissed each other. Truth shall spring out of the earth: and Righteousness shall look down from heaven. Yea, the Lord shall give that which is good; and our land shall yield her increase. Righteousness shall go before Him, and shall set us in the way of His steps." Now the Savior, while praying for His disciples, said: "Sanctify them through Thy truth—Thy word is truth." From these passages we learn, that His word is to spring out of the earth, while Righteousness looks down from heaven. And the next thing that follows is, that Israel are set in the way of His steps, and partaking of the fruit of their own land. Jeremiah, xxxiii, 6, speaking of the final return from captivity of both Judah and Israel, says: "I will reveal unto them the abundance of peace and truth." And Isaiah, speaking of the everlasting covenant, which should gather them, makes this extraordinary and very remarkable expression: "Their seed shall be known amongst the Gentiles, and their offspring among the people." Now, reader, let me ask, can any one tell whether the Indians of America are of Israel, unless by revelation from God? Therefore this was a hidden mystery, which it was necessary to reveal in time for their gathering.

So much, then, we have produced from the Scriptures, in proof of a work, like the book of Mormon, making its appearance in these days; to say nothing of Isaiah, xxix. But says one, "What is the use of the Book of Mormon, even if it be true?" I answer: First, it brings to light an important history, before unknown to man. Second, it reveals the origin of the American Indians, which was before a mystery. Third, it contains important prophecies, yet to be fulfilled, which immediately concern the present generation. Fourth, it contains much plainness in regard to points of doctrine, insomuch that all may understand, and see eye to eye, if they take pains to read it.

"But what are its proofs, as to chosen witnesses who testify to its translation by inspiration?" For this testimony, I refer the reader to the testimony of the witnesses in the first page of the Book of Mormon; he will there find as positive testimony as has ever been found in the other Scriptures concerning any truth which God ever revealed. Men there testify, not only that they have seen and handled the plates, but that an angel of God came down from heaven, and presented the plates before them, while the glory of God shone round about them, and the voice of God spoke from heaven, and told them that these things were true, and had been translated by the gift and power of God, and commanded them to bear record of the same to all people.

Blessed be the Lord God of our fathers! He has visited His people, and the dayspring from on high has dawned upon our benighted world once more; for no sooner had the Book been translated, and men begun to bear record of the same, than the Angel of the Lord came down from heaven again, and commissioned men to preach the Gospel to every creature, and to baptize with water for the remission of sins. No sooner did the people begin to believe their testimony, and be baptized, than the Holy Ghost fell upon them, through the laying on of hands in the name of Jesus; and the heavens were opened: and while some had the ministering of angels, others began to speak in other tongues, and prophesy. From that time forth, many of them were healed by the laying on of hands in the name of Jesus; and thus mightily grew the word of God, and prevailed. And thus, thousands have been raised up to testify that they do know for themselves, and are not dependent on the testimony of any man, for the truth of these things, for these signs follow them that believe. And when a man believes the truth, through the testimony of God's witnesses, and then these signs follow, not only them, but him also; if he has the ministering of angels, if he has been healed, or heals others, by the laying on of hands in the name of Jesus, or if he speaks in other tongues, or prophesies, he knows it for himself; and thus is fulfilled the saying of Scripture, "If any man do my will, he shall know of the doctrine, whether it be of God." Thus faith comes by hearing, and knowledge by obeying; but hearing comes by preaching, and preaching comes by sending; as it is written — "How shall they preach, except they be sent?"

But there are many who say — "Show us a sign, and we will believe." Remember, faith comes not by signs, but signs come by faith. Gifts were not given to make men believe; but what saith the Scripture? "Gifts are for the edifying of the Church." If otherwise, why was it not written — "Faith comes by miracles," instead of "Faith comes by hearing?" I always take it for granted, that a man or woman who comes demanding a sign in order to make them believe, belongs to a wicked and adulterous generation, at least, to say no worse; for any person who will go to Jesus, with a pure heart, desiring and praying in faith, that he may know the truth concerning these things, the Lord will reveal it to him, and he shall know, and shall bear testimony, for by the Spirit of God they shall know truth from error: as it is written—"My sheep hear my voice." And he that will not come unto Jesus by faith, shall never know the truth, until, too late, he finds the harvest is over, and the summer is ended, and his soul not saved.

Thus the religion of Jesus, unlike all other religious systems, bears its own weight, and brings certainty and knowledge, leaving no room for imposition. And now I say unto all people, Come unto the Father in the name of Jesus; doubt not, but be believing, as in days of old, and ask in faith for whatsoever you stand in need of; ask not that you may consume it on your lusts, but ask with a firmness not to be shaken, that you will yield to no temptation, but that you will keep His commandments, as fast as He makes them manifest unto you; and if ye do this, and He reveals to you that He has sent us with a new and everlasting covenant, and commanded us to preach, and baptize, and build up His Church as in days of old, then come forward and obey the truth; but if you do not know, or are not satisfied that He has sent us, then do not embrace the doctrine we preach. Thus to your own master you shall stand or fall; and one day you shall know, yea, in that great day, when every knee shall bow, then shall you know that God has sent us with the truth, to prune His vineyard for the last time, with a mighty pruning.

We shall now introduce much circumstantial evidence, from American antiquities, and from the traditions of the natives, etc.

First, says Mr. Boudinot: "It is said among their principal or beloved men, that they have it handed down from their ancestors, that the book which the white people have, was once theirs: that while they had it they prospered exceedingly, etc. They also say, that their fathers were possessed of an extraordinary Divine Spirit, by which they foretold future events, and controlled the common course of nature; and this they transmitted to their offspring, on condition of their obeying the sacred laws; that they did, by these means, bring down showers of blessings upon their beloved people; but that this power, for a long time past, had entirely ceased." Colonel James Smith, in his journal, while a prisoner among the natives, says: "They have a tradition, that in the beginning of this continent, the angels or heavenly inhabitants, as they call them, frequently visited the people, and talked with their forefathers, and gave directions how to pray."

Mr. Boudinot, in his able work, remarks concerning their language: "Their language, in its roots, idiom, and particular construction, appears to have the whole genius of the Hebrew; and what is very remarkable, and well worthy of serious attention, has most of the peculiarities of that language." There is a tradition related by an aged

Indian, of the Stockbridge tribe, that their fathers were once in possession of a "Sacred Book," which was handed down from generation to generation; and at last hid in the earth, since which time they had been under the feet of their enemies. But these oracles were to be restored to them again; and then they would triumph over their enemies, and regain their rights and privileges. Mr. Boudinot, after recording many traditions similar to the above, at length remarks: "Can any man read this short account of Indian traditions, drawn from tribes of various nations; from the west to the east, and from the south to the north, wholly separated from each other, written by different authors of the best character, both for knowledge and integrity, possessing the best means of information, at various and distant times, without any possible communication with each other; and yet suppose that all this is the effect of chance, accident, or design, from a love of the marvelous, or a premeditated intention of deceiving, and thereby ruining their well established reputation? Can any one carefully, and with deep reflection, consider and compare these traditions and nations with the position and circumstances of the long lost ten tribes of Israel, without at least drawing some presumptive inferences in favor of these wandering natives being descended from the ten tribes of Israel?"

"Joseph Merrick, Esq., a highly respectable character in Pitsfield, Mass., gave the following account: That in 1815, he was leveling some ground under and near an old wood-shed standing on a place of his, situated on Indian Hill. He ploughed and conveyed away old chips and earth to some depth. After the work was done, walking over the place, he discovered, near where the earth had been dug the deepest, a black strap, as it appeared, about six inches in length, and one and a half in breadth, and about the thickness of a leather trace to a harness. He perceived it had, at each end, a loop of some hard substance, probably for the purpose of carrying it. He conveyed it to his house, and threw it into an old tool box. He afterwards found it thrown out at the door, and again conveyed it to the box.

"After some time, he thought he would examine it; but in attempting to cut it, found it as hard as bone; he succeeded, however, in getting it open, and found it was formed of two pieces of thick rawhide, sewed and made water-tight with the sinews of some animal, and gummed over; and in the fold was contained four folded pieces of parchment. They were of a dark yellow hue, and contained some kind of writing. The neighbors coming in to see the strange discovery, tore one of the pieces to atoms, in the true Hun and Vandal style. The other three pieces Mr. Merrick saved, and sent them to Cambridge, where they were examined, and discovered to have been written with a pen, in Hebrew, plain and legible. The writing on the three remaining pieces of parchment, was quotations from the Old Testament. See Deut., vi, from 4−9; also xi, 13−21; and Exodus, xiii, 11−16, to which the reader can refer, if he has the curiosity to read this most interesting discovery.

"On the banks of White River, in Arkansas Territory, have been found ruins erected no doubt by an enlightened population, of the most extraordinary character, on account of their dimensions, and the materials of which they were erected. One of these works is a wall of earth, which encloses an area of six hundred and forty acres, equal to a mile square, and having, in its centre, the foundation of a large circular building, or temple. Another, yet more strange, and more extensive, consists of the foundations of a great city, whose streets, crossing each other at right angles, are easily traced through the mighty forest. And besides these are found the foundations of houses, made of burnt bricks, like the bricks of the present time. These have been traced to the extent of a mile."

The foregoing is taken from Priest's American Antiquities, and from the same work we extract the following, page 246:

"Ruins of the City of Otolum, discovered in North America. — In a letter of C. S. Rafinesque, whom we have before quoted, to a correspondent in Europe, we find the following: 'Some years ago, the Society of Geography, in Paris, offered a large premium for a voyage to Guatemala, and for a new survey of the antiquities of Yucatan and Chiapa, chiefly those fifteen miles from Palenque.'"

"I have," says this author, "restored to them the true name of Otolum, which is yet the name of the stream running through the ruins. They were surveyed by Captain Del Rio, in 1787, an account of which was published in English, in 1822. This account describes partly the ruins of a stone city, of no less dimensions than seventy-five miles in circuit; length, thirty-two, and breadth twelve miles, full of palaces, monuments, statues, and inscriptions: one of the earliest seats of American civilization; about equal to Thebes of ancient Egypt."

It is stated in the Family Magazine, No. 34, p. 266, for 1833, as follows: "Public attention has been recently excited, respecting the ruins of an ancient city, found in Guatemala. It would seem that these ruins are now being explored, and much curious and valuable matter, in a literary and historical point of view, is anticipated. We deem the present a most auspicious moment, now that the public attention is turned to the subject, to spread its contents before our readers, as an introduction to future discoveries, during the researches now in progress."

The following are some of the particulars, as related by Captain Del Rio, who partially examined them, as above related, in 1787: "From Palenque, the last town northward in the province of Ciudad Real de Chiapa, taking a southwesterly direction, and ascending a ridge of high land, that divides the kingdom of Guatemala from Yucatan, at the distance of six miles, is the little river Micol, whose waters flow in a westerly direction, and unite with the great river Tulijah, which bends its course towards the province of Tobasco. Having passed Micol, the ascent begins, and at half a league, or a mile and a half, the traveler crosses a little stream called Otolum; from this point heaps of stone ruins are discovered, which render the roads very difficult for another half league, when you gain the height whereon the stone houses are situated, being still fourteen in number in one place, some more dilapidated than others, yet still having many of their apartments perfectly discernible. These stand on a rectangular area, three hundred yards in breadth by four hundred and fifty in length, which is a fraction over fifty-six rods wide, and eighty-four rods long, being in the whole circuit, two hundred and eighty rods, which is three fourths of a mile, and a trifle over. This area presents a plain at the base of the highest mountain forming the ridge. In the centre of this plain is situated the largest of the structures which has been, as yet, discovered among these ruins. It stands on a mound, or pyramid, twenty yards high, which is sixty feet, or nearly four rods, in perpendicular altitude, which gives it a lofty and beautiful majesty, as if it were a temple suspended in the sky. This is surrounded by other edifices, namely, five to the northward, four to the southward, one to the southwest, and three to the eastward, fourteen in all.

"In all directions, the fragments of other fallen buildings are seen extending along the mountain, that stretches east and west either way from these buildings, as if it were the great temple of worship, or their government-house, around which they built their city, and where dwelt their kings and officers of state. At this place was found a subterranean stone aqueduct, of great solidity and durability, which in its course passes beneath the largest building."

Let it be understood, this city of Otolum, the ruins of which are so immense, is in North, not South America, in the same latitude with the island of Jamaica, which is about eighteen degrees north of the equator, being on the highest ground between the northern end of the Caribbean Sea and the Pacific Ocean, where the continent narrows towards the Isthmus of Darien, and is about eight hundred miles south of New Orleans.

The discovery of these ruins, and also of many others, equally wonderful, in the same country, is just commencing to arouse the attention of the schools of Europe, which hitherto have denied that America could boast of her antiquities. But these immense ruins are now being explored under the direction of scientific persons, a history of which, in detail, will, doubtless, be forthcoming in due time; two volumes of which, in manuscript, we are informed, have already been written, and cannot but be received with enthusiasm by Americans.

A gentleman who was living near the town of Cincinnati, in 1826, on the upper level, had occasion to sink a well for his accommodation; he persevered in digging to the depth of eighty feet, without finding water; but still persisting in the attempt, his workmen found themselves obstructed by a substance, which resisted their labor, though evidently not stone. They cleared the surface and sides from the earth bedded around it, when there appeared the stump of a tree, three feet in diameter, and two feet high, which had been cut down with an ax. The blows of the ax were yet visible. It was nearly of the color and apparent character of coal, but had not the friable and fusible quality of that substance. Ten feet below, the water sprang up, and the well is now in constant supply and high repute.

In Morse's Universal Geography, first volume, p. 142, the discovery of the stump is corroborated: "In digging a well in Cincinnati, the stump of a tree was found in a sound state, ninety feet below the surface; and in digging another well, at the same place, another stump was found, at ninety four feet below the surface, which had evident marks of the ax; and on its top there appeared as if some iron tool had been consumed by rust."

We might fill a volume with accounts of American antiquities, all going to show that this country has been inhabited by a people who possessed a knowledge of the arts and sciences, who built cities, cultivated the earth, and who were in possession of a written language. But the things which we have here introduced are abundantly sufficient for our purpose. If a few characters in Hebrew have been found in the earth in America, written on parchment, then it is just as easy to admit that a whole volume has been found in the earth in America, written on plates, in Egyptian characters. The astonishing facts of the stumps found eighty or ninety feet under ground at Cincinnati, and similar discoveries in many other parts of North and South America, such as buried cities, and other antiquities, all go to prove that there has been a mighty convulsion and revolution, not only of nations, but of nature; and such a convulsion as is nowhere else so reasonably accounted for, as in the following extraordinary and wonderful account of events, which transpired in this country, during the crucifixion of Messiah, which we extract from the Book of Mormon, Nephi, v, 2-11:

"And it came to pass, in the thirty and fourth year, in the first month, in the fourth day of the month, there arose a great storm, such an one as never had been known in all the land; and there was also a great and terrible tempest; and there was terrible thunder, insomuch that it did shake the whole earth, as if it was about to divide asunder; and there were exceeding sharp lightnings, such as never had been known in all the land. And the city of Zarahemla did take fire; and the city of Moroni did sink into the depths of the sea, and the inhabitants thereof were drowned; and the earth was carried up upon the city of Moronihah, that, in the place of the city thereof, there became a great mountain; and there was a great and terrible destruction in the land southward. But, behold, there was a more great and terrible destruction in the land northward; for, behold, the whole face of the land was changed, because of the tempest, and the whirlwinds, and the thunderings, and the lightnings, and the exceeding great quaking of the whole earth; and the highways were broken up, and the level roads were spoiled, and many smooth places became rough, and many great and notable cities were sunk, and many were burned, and many were shook till the buildings thereof had fallen to the earth, and the inhabitants thereof were slain, and the places were left desolate; and there were some cities which remained, but the damage thereof was exceeding great, and there were many in them who were slain, and there were some who were carried away in the whirlwind, and whither they went, no man knoweth, save they know that they were carried away; and thus the face of the whole earth became deformed, because of the tempests, and the thunderings, and the lightnings, and the quaking of the earth. And, behold, the rocks were rent in twain; they were broken up upon the face of the whole earth, insomuch that they were found in broken fragments, and in seams, and in cracks, upon all the face of the land.

"And it came to pass, that when the thunderings, and the lightnings, and the storm, and the tempest, and the quakings of the earth did cease—for, behold, they did last for about the space of three hours: and it was said by some that the time was greater; nevertheless, all these great and terrible things were done in about the space of three hours; and then, behold, there was darkness upon the face of the land.

"And it came to pass that there was a thick darkness upon all the face of the land, insomuch that the inhabitants thereof, who had not fallen, could feel the vapor of darkness; and there could be no light because of the darkness, neither candles, neither torches; neither could there be fire kindled with their fine and exceeding dry wood, so that there could not be any light at all; and there was not any light seen, neither fire, nor glimmer, neither the sun, nor the moon, nor the stars, for so great were the mists of darkness which were upon the face of the land.

"And it came to pass, that it did last for the space of three days, that there was no light seen; and there was great mourning and howling, and weeping among all the people continually; yea, great were the groanings of the people, because of the darkness and great destruction which had come upon them. And in one place they were heard to cry, saying, O that we had repented before this great and terrible day, and then would our brethren have been spared, and they would not have been burned in that great city of Zarahemla! And in another place they were heard to cry and mourn, saying, O that we had repented before this great and terrible day, and had not killed and Stoned the prophets and cast them out; then would our mothers, and our fair daughters, and our children have been spared, and not have been buried up in that great city Moronihah; and thus were the howlings of the people great and terrible.

"And it came to pass, that there was a voice heard among all the inhabitants of the earth upon the face of this land, crying, Wo, wo, wo unto this people; wo unto the inhabitants of the whole earth, except they shall repent, for the devil laugheth, and his angels rejoice, because of the slain of the fair sons and daughters of my people; and it is because of their iniquity and abominations that they are fallen. Behold, that great city of Zarahemla have I burned with fire, and the inhabitants thereof. And behold, that great city Moroni have I caused to be sunk in the depth of the sea, and the inhabitants thereof to be drowned. And behold, that great city Moronihah have I covered with earth, and the inhabitants thereof, to hide their iniquities and their abominations from before my face, that the blood of the prophets and the saints shall not come any more unto me against them. And behold the city of Gilgal have I caused to be sunk, and the inhabitants thereof to be buried up in the depths of the earth: yea, and the city of Onihah and the inhabitants thereof, and the city of Mocum and the inhabitants thereof, and the city of Jerusalem and the inhabitants thereof, and waters have I caused to come up in the stead thereof, to hide their wickedness and abominations from before my face, that the blood of the prophets and the saints shall not come up any more unto me against them. And behold the city of Gadiandi, and the city of Gadiomnah, and the city of Jacob, and the city of Gimgimno, all these have I caused to be sunk, and made hills and valleys in the places thereof; and the inhabitants thereof have I buried up in the depths of the earth, to hide their wickedness and abominations from before my face, that the blood of the prophets and saints should not come up anymore unto me against them. And behold that great city of Jacobugath, which was inhabited by the people of the king of Jacob, have I caused to be burned with fire, because of their sins and their wickedness, which was above all the wickedness of the whole earth, because of their secret murders and combinations; for it was they that did destroy the peace of my people and the government of the land: therefore I did cause them to be burned, to destroy them from before my face, that the blood of the prophets and the saints should not come up unto me any more against them. And behold, the city of Laman, and the city of Josh, and the city of Gad, and tho city of Kishkumen, have I caused to be burned with fire, and the inhabitants thereof, because of their wickedness in casting out the prophets, and stoning those whom I did send to declare unto them concerning their wickedness and their abominations; and because they did cast them all out, that there were none righteous among them, I did send down fire and destroy them, that their wickedness and abominations might be hid from before my face, that the blood of the prophets and the saints whom I sent among them might not cry unto me from the ground against them; and many great destructions have I caused to come upon this land and upon this people, because of their wickedness and their abominations.

"O, all ye that are spared, because ye were more righteous than they, will ye not now return unto me, and repent of your sins, and be converted, that I may heal you? Yea, verily, I say unto you, if ye will come unto me, ye shall have eternal life. Behold, mine arm of mercy is extended towards you, and whomsoever will come, him will I receive; and blessed are those who come unto me. Behold, I am Jesus Christ, the son of God. I created the heavens and the earth, and all things that in them are. I was with the Father from the beginning. I am in the Father, and the Father in me; and in me hath the Father glorified his name. I came unto my own, and my own received me not. And the Scriptures concerning my coming are fulfilled. And as many as have received me, to them have I given to become the sons of God; and even so will I to as many as shall believe on my name; for, behold, by me redemption cometh, and in me is the law of Moses fulfilled. I am the light and life of the world. I am Alpha and Omega, the beginning and the end. And ye shall offer up unto me no more the shedding of blood: yea, your sacrifices and your burnt offerings shall be done away, for I will accept none of your sacrifices and your burnt offerings; and ye shall offer, for a sacrifice unto me, a broken heart and a contrite spirit. And whoso cometh unto me with a broken heart and a contrite spirit, him will I baptize with fire and with the Holy Ghost, even as the Lamanites, because of their faith in me, at the time of their conversion, were baptized with fire and with the Holy Ghost, and they knew it not. Behold, I have come unto the world to bring redemption unto the world, to save the world from sin: therefore, whoso repenteth and cometh unto me as a little child, him will I receive; for of such is the kingdom of God. Behold, for such I have laid down my life, and have taken it up again: therefore, repent and come unto me, ye ends of the earth, and be saved.

"And now, behold it came to pass, that all the people of the land did hear these sayings; and did witness of it. And after these sayings, there was silence in the land for the space of many hours: for so great was the astonishment of the people that they did cease lamenting and howling for the loss of their kindred which had been slain; therefore there was silence in all the land for the space of many hours.

"And it came to pass, that there came a voice again unto the people, and all the people did hear, and did witness of it, saying, O ye people of these great cities which have fallen, who are descendants of Jacob; yea, who are of the house of Israel, how oft have I gathered you as a hen gathereth her chickens under her wings, and have nourished you. And again, how oft would I have gathered you, as a hen gathereth her chickens under her wings; yea, O ye people of the house of Israel, who have fallen; yea, O ye people of the house of Israel; ye that dwell at Jerusalem, as ye that have fallen; yea, how oft would I have gathered you, as a hen gathereth her chickens, and ye would not. O, ye house of Israel, whom I have spared, how oft will I gather you, as a hen gathereth her chickens under her wings, if ye will repent and return unto me with full purpose of heart. But if not, O house of Israel, the places of your dwellings shall become desolate, until the time of the fulfilling of the covenant to your fathers.

"And now it came to pass, that after the people had heard these words, behold, they began to weep and howl again, because of the loss of their kindred and friends. And it came to pass that thus did three days pass away. And it was in the morning, and the darkness dispersed from off the face of the land, and the earth did cease to tremble, and the rocks did cease to rend, and the dreadful groanings did cease, and all the tumultuous noises did pass away, and the earth did cleave together again, that it stood; and the mourning, and the weeping, and the wailing of the people who were spared alive, did cease, and their mourning was turned into joy, and their lamentations into the praise and thanksgiving unto the Lord Jesus Christ, their Redeemer. And thus far were the Scriptures fulfilled, which had been spoken by the prophets."

Here, then, is an account which shows, clearly and definitely, how and when the American antiquities became buried; how the stumps of trees were placed eighty or ninety feet under ground; how cities were sunk, and overwhelmed; how mountains fell and valleys rose; how the rocks were rent, and how the whole face of the continent became altered and deformed. We now close this subject by saying to all the people, if you wish information on the antiquities of America; if you wish historical, prophetical, or doctrinal information of the highest importance, read carefully the Book of Mormon.

CHAPTER V

THE RESURRECTION OF THE SAINTS, AND THE RESTORATION OF ALL THINGS SPOKEN BY THE PROPHETS

This is one of the most important subjects upon which the human mind can contemplate; and one perhaps as little understood, in the present age, as any other now lying over the face of prophecy. But, however neglected at the present time, it was once the groundwork of the faith, hope, and joy of the Saints. It was a correct understanding of this subject, and firm belief in it, that influenced all their movements. Their minds once fastening upon it, they could not be shaken from their purposes; their faith was firm, their joy constant, and their hope like an anchor to the soul, both sure and steadfast, reaching to that within the veil. It was this that enabled them to rejoice in the midst of tribulation, persecution, sword, and flame; and in view of this, they took joyfully the spoiling of their goods, and gladly wandered as strangers and pilgrims on the earth. For they sought a country, a city, and an inheritance that none but a saint ever thought of, understood, or even hoped for.

Now, we can never understand precisely what is meant by restoration, unless we understand what is lost or taken away; for instance, when we offer to restore anything to a man, it is as much as to say he once possessed it, but had lost it, and we propose to replace, or put him in possession of, that which he once had; therefore, when a Prophet speaks of the restoration of all things, he means that all things have undergone a change, and are to be again restored to their primitive order, even as they first existed.

First, then, it becomes necessary to take a view of creation, as it rolled in purity from the hand of its Creator; and if we can discover the true state in which it then existed, and understand the changes that have taken place since, then we shall be able to understand what is to be restored; and thus, our minds being prepared, we shall be looking for the very things which will come, and shall be in no danger of lifting our puny arm in ignorance, to oppose the things of God. First, then, we will take a view of the earth, as to its surface, local situation, and productions.

When God had created the heavens and the earth, and separated the light from the darkness, His next great command was to the waters, Genesis, i, 9: "And God said, Let the waters under the heaven, be gathered together into one place, and let the dry land appear: and it was so." From this we learn a marvelous fact, which very few have ever realized or believed in this benighted age; we learn that the waters, which are now divided into oceans, seas, and lakes, were then all gathered together, into one vast ocean; and, consequently, that the land, which is now torn asunder, and divided into continents and islands, almost innumerable, was then one vast continent or body, not separated as it now is.

Second, we hear the Lord God pronounce the earth, as well as everything else, very good. From this we learn that there were neither deserts, barren places, stagnant swamps, rough, broken, rugged hills; nor vast mountains covered with eternal snow; and no part of it was located in the frigid zone, so as to render its climate dreary and unproductive, subject to eternal frost, or everlasting chains of ice —

Where no sweet flowers the dreary landscape cheer,

Nor plenteous harvests crown the passing year.

But the whole earth was probably one vast plain, or interspersed with gently rising hills, and sloping vales, well calculated for cultivation; while its climate was delightfully varied, with the moderate changes of heat and cold, of wet and dry, which only tended to crown the varied year with the greater variety of productions, all for the good of man, animal, fowl, or creeping thing; while from the flowery plain or spicy grove, sweet odors were wafted on every breeze; and all the vast creation of animated being breathed naught but health, and peace, and joy.

Next, we learn from Genesis, i, 29, 30: "And God said, Behold, I have given you every herb bearing seed, which is upon the face of all the earth, and every tree, in which is the fruit of a tree, yielding seed; to you it shall be for meat. And to every beast of the earth, and to every fowl of the air, and to everything that creepeth upon the earth, wherein there is life, I have given every green herb for meat: and it was so." From these verses we learn, that the earth yielded neither nauseous weeds nor poisonous plants, nor useless thorns and thistles; indeed every thing that grew was just calculated for the food of man, beast, fowl, and creeping thing; and their food was all vegetable. Flesh and blood were never sacrificed to glut their souls, or gratify their appetites; the beasts of the earth were all in perfect harmony with each other; the lion ate straw like the ox, the wolf dwelt with the lamb, the leopard lay down with the kid, the cow and bear fed together, in the same pasture, while their young ones reposed, in perfect security, under the shade of the same trees; all was peace and harmony, and nothing to hurt nor disturb, in all the holy mountain.

And to crown the whole, we behold man created in the image of God, and exalted in dignity and power, having dominion over all the vast creation of animated beings, which swarmed through the earth, while, at the same time, he inhabits a beautiful and well watered garden, in the midst of which stood the tree of life, to which he had free access; while he stood in the presence of his Maker, conversed with Him face to face, and gazed upon His glory, without a dimming veil between. O reader, contemplate, for a moment, the beautiful creation, clothed with peace and plenty; the earth teeming with harmless animals, rejoicing over all the plain; the air swarming with delightful birds, whose never-ceasing notes filled the air with varied melody; and all in subjection to their rightful sovereign, who rejoiced over them; while in a delightful garden—the capitol of creation, man was seated on the throne of this vast empire, swaying his sceptre over all the earth with undisputed right; while legions of angels encamped round about him, and joined their glad voices in grateful songs of praise, and shouts of joy; neither a sigh nor groan was heard throughout the vast expanse; neither were there sorrow, tears, pain, weeping, sickness, nor death; neither contentions, wars, nor bloodshed; but peace crowned the seasons as they rolled, and life, joy, and love reigned over all God's works. But, O, how changed the scene!

It now becomes my painful duty to trace some of the important changes which have taken place, and the causes which have conspired to reduce the earth and its inhabitants to their present state.

First, man fell from his standing before God, by giving heed to temptation; and this fall affected the whole creation, as well as man, and caused various changes to take place; he was banished from the presence of his Creator, and a veil was drawn between them, and man was driven from the garden of Eden, to till the earth, which was then cursed for his sake, and should begin to bring forth thorns and thistles; and with the sweat of his face he should earn his bread, and in sorrow eat of it, all the days of his life, and finally return to dust. But as to Eve, her curse was a great multiplicity of sorrow and conception; and between her seed and the seed of the serpent there was to be a constant enmity; it should bruise the serpent's head, and the serpent should bruise his heel.

Now, reader, contemplate the change. This scene, which was so beautiful a little before, had now become the abode of sorrow and toil, of death and mourning: the earth groaning with its production of accursed thorns and thistles; man and beast at enmity; the serpent slyly creeping away, fearing lest his head should get the deadly bruise; and man startling amid the thorny path, in fear, lest the serpent's fangs should pierce his heel; while the lamb yields his blood upon the smoking altar. Soon man begins to persecute, hate, and murder his fellow, until at length the earth is filled with violence, all flesh becomes corrupt, the powers of darkness prevail, and it repented Noah that God had made man, and it grieved him at his heart, because the Lord should come out in vengeance, and cleanse the earth by water.

How far the flood may have contributed to produce the various changes, as to the division of the earth into broken fragments, islands and continents, mountains and valleys, we have not been informed; the change must have been considerable. But after the flood, in the days of Peleg, the earth was divided. See Gen., x, 25. A short history, to be sure, of so great an event; but still it will account for the mighty revolution which rolled the sea from its own place in the north, and brought it to interpose between different portions of the earth, which were thus parted asunder, and moved into something near their present form; this, together with the earthquakes, revolutions, and commotions which have since taken place, have all contributed to reduce the face of the earth to its present state; while the great curses which have fallen upon different portions, because of the wickedness of men, will account for the stagnant swamps, the sunken lakes, the dead seas, the great deserts; witness, for instance, the denunciations of the Prophets upon Babylon, how it was to become perpetual desolations, a den of wild beasts, a dwelling of unclean and hateful birds, a place for owls; and should never be inhabited, but should lie desolate from generation to generation. Witness also the plains of Sodom, filled with towns, cities, and flourishing gardens, well watered; but O, how changed! A vast sea of stagnant water alone marks the place. Witness the land of Palestine; in the days of Solomon, it was capable of sustaining millions of people, besides yielding a surplus of wheat, and other productions, which were exchanged with the neighboring nations; whereas, now it is desolate, and hardly capable of sustaining a few miserable inhabitants. And when I cast mine eyes over our own land, and see the numerous swamps, lakes, and ponds of stagnant waters, together with the vast mountains, and innumerable rough places, rocks having been rent, and torn asunder, from centre to circumference, I exclaim, Whence all this?

When I read the Book of Mormon, it informs me, that while Christ was crucified among the Jews, this whole American continent was shaken to its foundation, that many cities were sunk, and waters came up in their places; that the rocks were all rent in twain; that mountains were thrown up to an exceeding height; and that other mountains became valleys; the level roads spoiled, and the whole face of the land changed. I then exclaim, These things are no longer a mystery; I have now learned to account for the many wonders, which I everywhere behold, throughout our whole country. When I am passing a ledge of rocks, and see they have all been rent and torn asunder, while some huge fragments are found deeply imbedded in the earth, some rods from whence they were torn, I exclaim, with astonishment, These were the groans! the convulsive throes of agonizing nature! while the Son of God suffered upon the cross!

But men have degenerated, and greatly changed, as well as the earth. The sins, the abominations, and the many evil habits of the latter ages, have added to the miseries, toils, and sufferings of human life. The idleness, extravagance, pride, covetousness, drunkenness, and other abominations, which are characteristics of the latter times, have all combined to sink mankind to the lowest state of wretchedness and degradation; while priestcraft and false doctrines have greatly tended to lull mankind to sleep, and cause them to rest infinitely short of the powers and attainments which the ancients enjoyed, and which are alone calculated to exalt the intellectual powers of the human mind, to establish noble and generous sentiments, to enlarge the heart, and to expand the soul to the utmost extent of its capacity. Witness the ancients conversing with the Great Jehovah, learning lessons from the angels, and receiving instruction by the Holy Ghost, in dreams by night, and visions by day, until at length the veil is taken off, and they are permitted to gaze, with wonder and admiration, upon all things past and future; yea, even to soar aloft amid unnumbered worlds, while the vast expanse of eternity stands open before them, and they contemplate the mighty works of the Great I AM, until they know as they are known, and see as they are seen.

Compare this intelligence with the low smatterings of education and worldly wisdom which seem to satisfy the narrow mind of man in our generation; yea, behold the narrow-minded, calculating, trading, overreaching, penurious sycophant of the nineteenth century, who dreams of nothing here, but how to increase his goods, or take advantage of his neighbor; and whose only religious exercise or duties consist of going to meeting, paying the priest his hire, or praying to his God, without expecting to be heard or answered, supposing that God has been deaf and dumb for many centuries, or altogether stupid and indifferent like himself. And having seen the two contrasted, you will be able to form some idea of the vast elevation from which man has fallen; you will also learn how infinitely beneath his former glory and dignity he is now living, and your heart will mourn, and be exceedingly sorrowful, when you contemplate him in his low estate — and then think he is your brother; and you will be ready to exclaim, with wonder and astonishment: "O man! how art thou fallen! Once thou wast the favorite of heaven; thy Maker delighted to converse with thee, and angels, and the spirits of just men made perfect, were thy companions; but now thou art degraded, and brought down to a level with the beasts; yea, far beneath them, for they look with horror and affright at your vain amusements, your sports, and your drunkenness, and thus often set an example worthy of your imitation. Well did the Apostle Peter say of you, that you know nothing, only what you know naturally as brute beasts, made to be taken and destroyed. And thus you perish, from generation to generation, while all creation groans under its pollution; and sorrow and death, mourning and weeping, fill up the measure of the days of man!" But, O my soul, dwell no longer on this awful scene! let it suffice to have discovered, in some degree, what is lost. Let us turn our attention to what the Prophets have said should be restored.

The Apostle Peter, while preaching to the Jews, says: "And He shall send Jesus Christ, which before was preached unto you, whom the heavens must receive, until the times of the restitution (restoration) of all things which God hath spoken, by the mouth of all His holy prophets since the world began." It appears from the above, that all the holy Prophets from Adam to Christ, and those that followed after, had their eyes upon a certain time, when all things should be restored to their primitive beauty and excellence. We also learn, that the time of restitution was to be at or near the time of Christ's second coming; for the heavens are to receive Him, until the times of restitution, and the Father shall send Him again to the earth.

We will now proceed to notice Isaiah, xl, 1-5. "Comfort ye, comfort ye my people, saith your God. Speak ye comfortably to Jerusalem, and cry unto her, that her warfare is accomplished, that her iniquity is pardoned; for she hath received of the Lord's hand, double for all her sins. The voice of him that crieth in the wilderness, Prepare ye the way of the Lord, make straight in the desert a highway for our God. Every valley shall be exalted, and every mountain and hill shall be made low; and the crooked shall be made straight, and the rough places plain; and tho glory of the Lord shall be revealed, and all flesh shall see it together; for the mouth of the Lord hath spoken it."

From these verses we learn, first, that the voice of one shall be heard in the wilderness, to prepare the way of the Lord, just at tho time when Jerusalem has been trodden down of the Gentiles long enough to have received, at the Lord's hand, double for all her sins, yea, when the warfare of Jerusalem is accomplished, and her iniquities pardoned. Then shall this proclamation be made as it was before by John, yea, a second proclamation, to prepare the way of the Lord, for His second coming; and about that time every valley shall exalted, and every mountain and hill shall be made low, and the crooked shall be made straight, and the rough places plain, and then the glory of the Lord shall be revealed, and all flesh shall see it together, for the mouth of the Lord hath spoken it.

Thus you see, every mountain being made low, and every valley exalted, and the rough places being made plain, and the crooked places straight—that these mighty revolutions will begin to restore the face of the earth to its former beauty. But all this done, we have not yet gone through our restoration; there are many more great things to be done in order to restore all things.

Our next, is Isaiah, twenty-fifth chapter, where we again read of the Lord's second coming, and of the mighty works which attend it. The barren desert should abound with pools and springs of living water, and should produce grass, with flowers blooming and blossoming as the rose, and that, too, about the time of the coming of their God, with vengeance and recompense, which must allude to His second coming; and Israel is to come at the same time to Zion, with songs of everlasting joy, and sorrow and sighing shall flee away. Here, then, we have the curse taken off the deserts, and they becomes fruitful, well-watered country.

We will now inquire whether the islands return again to the continents, from whence they were separated. For this subject we refer you to Revelations, vi, 14. "And every mountain and island were moved out of their places." From this we learn that they moved somewhere; and as it is the time of restoring what has been lost, they accordingly return and join themselves to the land whence they came.

Our next is Isaiah, xiii, 13, 14, where "The earth shall remove out of her place, And shall be as the chased roe, which no man taketh up." Also Isaiah, lxii, 4: "Thou shalt no more be termed Forsaken; neither shall thy land any more be termed Desolate; but thou shalt be called Hephzibah, and thy land Beulah; for the Lord delighteth in thee, and thy land shall be married."

In the first instance, we have the earth on a move like a chased roe; and in the second place, we have it married. And from the whole, and various Scriptures, we learn, that the continents and islands shall be united in one, as they were on the morn of creation, and the sea shall retire and assemble in its own place, where it was before; and all these scenes shall take place during the mighty convulsion of nature, about the time of the coming of the Lord.

> Behold! the mount of Olives rent in twain:
>
> While on its top He sets His feet again,
>
> The islands, at His word, obedient, flee;
>
> While to the north He rolls the mighty sea;
>
> Restores the earth in one, as at the first,
>
> With all its blessings, and removes the curse.

Having restored the earth to the same glorious state in which it first existed — leveling the mountains, exalting the valleys, smoothing the rough places, making the deserts fruitful, and bringing all the continents and islands together, causing the curse to be taken off, that noxious weeds, and thorns, and thistles shall no longer be produced; the next thing is to regulate and restore the brute creation to their former state of peace and glory, causing all enmity to cease from off the earth. But this will never be done until there is a general destruction poured out upon man, which will entirely cleanse the earth, and sweep all wickedness from its face. This will be done by the rod of His mouth, and by the breath of His lips; or, in other words, by fire as universal as the flood. Isaiah xi, 4, 6-9: "But with righteousness shall He judge the poor, and reprove with equity for the meek of the earth; and He shall smite the earth with the rod of His mouth, and with the breath of His lips shall He slay the wicked. The wolf also shall dwell with the lamb, and the leopard shall lie down with the kid; and the calf and the young lion, and the falling together; and a little child shall lead them. And the cow and the bear shall feed; their young ones shall lie down together; and the lion shall eat straw like the ox. And the suckling child shall play on the hole of the asp, and the weaned child shall put his hand on the cockatrice's den. They shall not hurt nor destroy in all my holy mountain; for the earth shall be full of the knowledge of the Lord, as the waters cover the sea."

Thus, having cleansed the earth, and glorified it with the knowledge of God, as the waters cover the sea, and having poured out His Spirit upon all flesh, both man and beast becoming perfectly harmless, as they were in the beginning, and feeding on vegetable food only, while nothing is left to hurt or destroy in all the vast creation, the Prophets then proceed to give us many glorious descriptions of the enjoyments of its inhabitants. "They shall build houses and inhabit them; and they shall plant vineyards and eat the fruit of them; they shall not build and another inhabit; they shall not plant and another eat; for as the days of a tree are the days of my people, and mine elect shall long enjoy the work of their hands. They shall not labor in vain, nor bring forth for trouble; for they are the seed of the blest of the Lord, and their offspring with them; and it shall come to pass, that before they call I will answer, and while they are yet speaking I will hear." In this happy state of existence it seems that all people will live to the full age of a tree, and this, too, without pain or sorrow, and whatsoever they ask will be immediately answered, and even all their wants will be anticipated. Of course, then, none of them will sleep in the dust, for they will prefer to be translated, that is, changed in the twinkling of an eye, from mortal to immortal; after which they will continue to reign with Jesus on the earth.

Thus we have traced the Prophets through the varying scenes which conspire to restore the earth, and its inhabitants, to that state of perfection in which they first existed, and in which they will exist during the great Sabbath of creation. Having seen all things restored among the living, we will now inquire after those who sleep in the dust; but, in order to understand precisely the nature of their restoration, we must ascertain the particulars concerning the resurrection of Jesus, for He was an exact pattern after which all His Saints will be raised. We recollect, first, that he was clothed upon with flesh, and blood, and bones, like another man, and every way subject to hunger, thirst, pain, weariness, sickness, and death, like any other person—with this difference, that He was capable of enduring more than any other human body. Second, this same body was hung upon the cross, torn with nails, which were driven through His hands and feet, and His side pierced with a spear, from which there came out blood and water. Third, this same body, being perfectly lifeless, like any other corpse, was taken, without a bone being broken, and carefully wrapped in linen and laid in the tomb, where it continued until the third day; when, early in the morning, the women came to the sepulchre, and His disciples also, and found the linen clothes lying useless, and the napkin which was about His head carefully folded and laid by itself, but the body which had lain there was gone.

From all these circumstances, we discover that the same flesh and bones which were laid in the tomb were actually re-animated, and did arise and lay aside the linen which was no longer needed. And Jesus Christ came forth triumphant from the mansions of the dead, possessing the same body which had been born of a woman, and which was crucified; but no blood flowed in His veins, for blood was the natural life, in which were the principles of mortality, and a man restored to flesh and blood would be mortal, and, consequently, again subject unto death, which was not the case with our Savior, although He had flesh and bones after He arose, for when He appeared to His disciples, and they were afraid, supposing it was only a spirit, in order to show them their mistake, He said: "Handle me and see, for a spirit hath not flesh and bones as ye see me have." And calling for something to eat, He was provided with a piece of broiled fish and honeycomb, and He did eat. And even afterwards, Thomas was invited to put his finger into the prints of the nails in His hands and feet, and to thrust his hand into His side, from which it was evident that He not only possessed the same body, but the same wounds also continued to show themselves for a witness, and will continue until He comes again, when the Jews will look upon Him whom they have pierced, and inquire, "What are these wounds in thy hands and in thy feet?"

O ye hard hearted, ye ungodly children of men! your eyes will very soon behold Him who was crucified for your sins; then shall ye see that the resurrection of the dead is a reality, something tangible, and that eternity is not a land of shades, nor a world of phantoms, as some suppose.

Among other things which Jesus did after the resurrection, we find Him in the humble attitude of broiling fish, and calling His disciples to come and dine. O what simplicity, what love, what condescension! Wonder, O heavens! Be astonished, O earth! Behold the Redeemer clothed upon with immortality, and yet seated by a fire of coals, in the open air, with His brethren, humbly partaking of a meal of fish, actually prepared by His own hands! O ye great and noble of the earth, who roll in luxury and refinement! O ye priests, who are loaded with the honors, titles, dignities, riches, and splendor of the world, here is a lesson for you, which will make you blush: boast no more of being followers of the meek and lowly Jesus!

But to return to the subject of the resurrection. Having proved to a demonstration, that our Savior rose from the dead, with the same body which was crucified — possessing flesh and bones, that He ate and drank with His disciples, it puts the matter forever at rest respecting the resurrection of the Saints. But if more proof were wanting, we have it in the prophecy of Job, quoted in a former part of this work, where he declares that his Redeemer will stand, in the latter-day, upon the earth, and he should see Him in the flesh, though worms should destroy the body which he then had. The fact is, the Saints will again receive their bodies, every joint being in its proper and perfect frame, and clothed upon with flesh, sinews, and skin, like as we now are; the whole being immortal, no more to see corruption, and clothed with a white robe of fine linen, suitable for immortality to wear. Well did the Apostle say, In heaven we have a more enduring substance (not shadow).

But in order to illustrate this subject still farther, we will carefully examine Ezekiel xxxvii, which we have touched upon before. In this vision, the Prophet is carried away in the Spirit, and a valley of dry bones is presented before him, and they are very numerous and very dry; and while he stands musing and contemplating the awful scene, a very wonderful question is proposed to him: "Son of man, can these dry bones live?" and he answered: "O Lord God, thou knowest." And the Lord said: "Son of man, prophesy upon these bones, and say, O ye dry bones, hear the word of the Lord." So he prophesied as he was commanded, and, as he prophesied, there was a noise, and behold, a shaking, and the bones came together, bone to his bone, and the sinews and the flesh came upon them, and the skin covered them. And again he prophesied to the winds, saying: "Come from the four winds, O breath, and breathe upon these slain, that they may live;" and the breath entered into them, and they lived and stood upon their feet, an exceeding great army. We have heard many comments upon this vision; some compare it to sinners being converted, and some to the body of Christ, the Church, when dead as to the spiritual gifts; but the Church becoming dead, can no longer be said to be the body of Christ, as when she abides in the true vine, she lives and bears fruit, and is not dead, and when she does not abide in Him, she is cut off as a branch withered, and burned, instead of rising again. But did you ever hear the Lord's own explanation of this vision, in the same chapter? It so far surpasses all other comments, I am inclined to believe it; I will therefore write it in preference to any other, and run the risk of becoming unpopular by so doing. The Lord says: "Son of man, these bones are the whole house of Israel; behold, they say, Our bones are dried, and our hope is lost: we are cut off for our parts. Therefore, prophesy and say unto them, Thus saith the Lord God, Behold, O my people, I will open your graves, and cause you to come up out of your graves, and bring you into the land of Israel: and ye shall know that I am the Lord, when I have opened your graves, O my people, and brought you up out of your graves, and shall put my Spirit in you, and ye shall live; and I shall place you in your own land. Then shall ye know that I the Lord have spoken it, and performed it, saith the Lord." Thus you have the whole vision unfolded plainly, if the Lord's authority can once be allowed, which is seldom the case in this age of wisdom and learning. The fact is, all the seed of Israel are to be raised from the dead, and are to be brought into the land of Israel, which was given to them for an everlasting inheritance. And in order to do this, their old dry bones are to be brought together, bone to its bone, and every part of their bodies is to be reinstated; and it will make a great noise, and a wonderful shaking when they come together; and surely when they stand upon their feet they will make an exceeding great army.

This just explains the promise, so oft repeated in Scripture: "My servant David shall be their prince for ever;" indeed this same chapter makes the promise to them, that His servant David shall be raised up, and shall be a prince among them, while the Lord shall be their King; while both they that are alive, and they that are dead, shall be restored, and become one nation, in the land, upon the mountains of Israel; while David comes forth and reigns as a prince and shepherd over them for ever; and the Lord Jesus reigns as King of kings, and Lord of lords, in Mount Zion, and in Jerusalem, and before His ancients gloriously.

O glorious day! O blessed hope!

My soul leaps forward at the thought;

When in that happy, happy land,

We'll take the ancients by the hand;

In love and union hail our friends;

And Death and Sorrow have an end.

I now no longer marvel, when I call to mind that Abraham counted himself a stranger and a pilgrim, seeking a better country, and a city whose builder and maker is God. It seems after this restoration there will be but one more change necessary, in order to fit the earth for man's eternal inheritance; and that change is to take place at the last day, after man has enjoyed it in peace a thousand years. We have now discovered the great secret, which none but the Saints have understood (but was well understood by them in all ages of the world), which is this, that man is to dwell in the flesh, upon the earth, with the Messiah, with the whole house of Israel, and with all the Saints of the Most High, not only one thousand years, but for ever and ever. There our father Adam, whose hair is white like the pure wool, will sit enthroned in dignity, as the Ancient of Days, the great Patriarch, the mighty Prince; while thousands of thousands stand before him, and ten thousand times ten thousand minister to him; there he will hail all his children, who died in the faith of the Messiah; while Abel, Enoch, Noah, Abraham, Job, and Daniel, with all the Prophets and Apostles, and all the Saints of God of all ages, hail each other in the flesh. Jesus, the great Messiah, will stand in the midst, and, to crown the whole, will gird himself, and administer bread and wine to the whole multitude, and He himself will partake of the same with them on the earth, all being clothed in fine linen, clean and white. This is the marriage supper of the Lamb, Blessed are they who partake thereof.

Having traced the great restoration of the earth and its inhabitants, until we find them in the full enjoyment of the promises made to their fathers; and having learned that a future state is not a state of shadows and fables, but something tangible, even a more enduring substance, we shall now take a view of the division of their land, and the laying out of their city, oven the holy city, where the tabernacle of God and His sanctuary shall be forevermore, for of course this was the city sought for by Abraham and others, who found it not.

This view is given in the last chapter of Ezekiel, where he divides the land, by lot, to the whole twelve tribes; and lays off the city, and sanctuary in the midst, with its twelve gates, three on each side, the whole lying four square. But in the forty-seventh chapter, we have a description of a beautiful river, which will issue forth from the eastern front of the temple, from under the sanctuary, and run eastward into the Dead Sea, healing the waters, and causing a very great, multitude of fishes; so that from Engedi, and Eneglaim, the fishers spread forth their nets; while the miry places shall not be healed, but shall be given to salt. And on either side shall grow all trees for meat, whose leaf shall not fade, nor shall the fruit thereof be consumed; it shall bring forth new fruit according to its months, because of the waters issuing from the sanctuary; and their fruits shall be for meat, and their leaves for medicine.

But to set forth more fully the building of the city, and the materials of which it will be built, we quote Isaiah, liv, 11, to the end of the chapter: "O thou afflicted, tossed with tempest, and not comforted, behold, I will lay thy stones with fair colors, and lay thy foundations with sapphires. And I will make thy windows of agates, and thy gates of carbuncles, and all thy borders of pleasant stones. And all thy children shall be taught of the Lord; and great shall be the peace of thy children. In righteousness shalt thou be established; thou shalt be far from oppression; for thou shalt not fear: and from terror; for it shall not come near thee. Behold, they shall surely gather together, but not by me: whosoever shall gather together, against thee shall fall for thy sake. Behold I have created the smith that bloweth the coals in the fire, and that bringeth forth an instrument for his work; and I have created the waster to destroy. No weapon that is formed against thee shall prosper; and every tongue that shall rise against thee in judgment thou shalt condemn. This is the heritage of the servants of the Lord, and their righteousness is of me, saith the Lord."

From these verses we learn something of the beauty of their city, and of the materials of which it is composed. Their stones of fair colors, their foundations of sapphires, their windows of agates, their gates of carbuncles, and all their borders of pleasant stones, are well calculated to beautify the place of His sanctuary, and to make the place of His feet glorious, as well as to give a lustre and magnificence to the whole city, of which the Gentiles, with all their boasted wealth and grandeur, can form but a faint idea; and then to mark, in the same description, the knowledge, as well as the peace and security, of all the inhabitants; while they who gather together against them to battle are sure to fall for their sake: surely this is the heritage of the servants of the Lord, surely this is a delightful city, and well worth a pilgrimage like Abraham's.

But in order to form a still more striking idea of the prosperity, wealth, beauty and magnificence of the cities of Zion and Jerusalem, we will quote Isaiah lx: "Arise, shine; for thy light is come, and the glory of the Lord is risen upon thee. For, behold, the darkness shall cover the earth, and gross darkness the people: but the Lord shall arise upon thee, and His glory shall be seen upon thee. And the Gentiles shall come to thy light, and kings to the brightness of thy rising. Lift up thine eyes, round about, and see; all they gather themselves together, they come to thee: thy sons shall come from far, and thy daughters shall be nursed at thy side. Thou thou shalt see, and flow together, and thine heart shall fear, and be enlarged; because the abundance of the sea shall be converted unto thee, the forces of the Gentiles shall come unto thee. The multitude of camels shall cover thee, the dromedaries of Midian and Epha; all they from Sheba shall come: they shall bring gold and incense; and they shall show forth the praises of the Lord. All the flocks of Kedar shall be gathered together unto thee, the rams of Nebaioth shall minister unto thee: they shall come up with acceptance on mine altar, and I will glorify the house of my glory. Who are these that fly as a cloud, and as the doves to their windows? Surely the isles shall wait for me, and the ships of Tarshish first, to bring thy sons from far, their silver and their gold with them, unto the name of the Lord thy God, and to the Holy One of Israel, because He hath glorified thee. And the sons of strangers shall build up thy walls, and their kings shall minister unto thee: for in my wrath I smote thee, but in my favor have I had mercy on thee. Therefore thy gates shall be open continually; they shall not be shut day nor night; that men may bring unto thee the forces of the

Gentiles, and that their kings may be brought. For the nation and kingdom that will not serve thee shall perish: yea, those nations shall be utterly wasted. The glory of Lebanon shall come unto thee, the fir-tree, the pine-tree, and the box together, to beautify the place of my sanctuary; and I will make the place of my feet glorious. The sons also of them that afflicted thee shall come bending unto thee; and all they that despised thee shall bow themselves down at the soles of thy feet; and they shall call thee, The city of the Lord, the Zion of the Holy One of Israel.

"Whereas thou hast been forsaken and hated, so that no man went through thee, I will make thee an eternal excellency, a joy of many generations. Thou shalt also suck the milk of the Gentiles, and shalt suck the breast of kings: and thou shalt know that I the Lord am thy Savior and thy Redeemer, the Mighty One of Jacob. For brass I will bring gold, and for iron I will bring silver, and for wood brass, and for stones iron: I will also make thy officers peace, and thine exactors righteousness. Violence shall no more be heard in thy land, wasting nor destruction within thy borders; but thou shalt call thy walls Salvation, and thy gates Praise. The sun shall be no more thy light by day; neither for brightness shall the moon give light unto thee: but the Lord shall be unto thee an everlasting light, and thy God thy glory. Thy sun shall no more go down; neither shall thy moon withdraw itself: for the Lord shall be thine everlasting light, and the days of thy mourning shall be ended. Thy people also shall be all righteous: they shall inherit the land for ever, the branch of my planting, the work of my hands, that I may be glorified. A little one shall become a thousand, and a small one a strong nation: I the Lord will hasten it in his time."

In this chapter we learn—First, that there is a city to be built in the last days, unto which, not only Israel, but all the nations of the Gentiles, are to flow; and the nation and kingdom that will not serve the city shall perish and be utterly wasted. Second, we learn that the name of that city is Zion, the city of the Lord. Third, we learn that it is called the place of His sanctuary, and the place of His feet. Fourth, that the best of timber, consisting of fir, pine, and boxwood, is to be brought in great plenty, to beautify the place of His sanctuary, and make the place of His feet glorious. Fifth, the precious metals are to abound in such plenty, that gold is to be in the room of brass, silver in the room of iron, brass in the room of wood, and iron in the room of stones. Their officers are to be peace officers, and their exactors righteous exactors; violence is no more to be heard in the land; wasting nor destruction within their borders. Their walls are to be Salvation, and their gates Praise: while the glory of God, in the midst of the city, outshines the sun. The days of their mourning are ended; their people are ail righteous, and are to inherit the land forever, being the branch of the Lord's planting, that He may be glorified. A little one shall become a strong nation, and the Lord will hasten it in His time.

The Psalmist David has told us, concerning the time of the building of this city, in his one hundred and second Psalm, from the thirteenth to the twenty-second verse: "Thou shalt arise and have mercy upon Zion; for the time to favor her, yea, the set time, is come. For Thy servants take pleasure in her stones, and favor the dust thereof. So the heathen shall fear the name of the Lord, and all the kings of the earth Thy glory. When the Lord shall build up Zion, He shall appear in His glory. He will regard the prayer of the destitute, and not despise their prayer. This shall be written for the generation to come: and the people which shall be created shall praise the Lord. For He hath looked down from the height of His sanctuary; from Heaven did the Lord behold the earth; to hear the groaning of the prisoner; to loose those that are appointed to death; to declare the name of the Lord in Zion, and His praise in Jerusalem; when the people are gathered together, and the kingdoms, to serve the Lord."

From this scripture we learn—First, that there is a set time to build up Zion, or the city of which Isaiah speaks, namely, just before the second coming of Christ; and that when this city is built, the Lord will appear in His glory, and not before. So from this we affirm, that if such a city is never built, then the Lord will never come. Second, we learn that the people and kingdoms are to be gathered together, to serve the Lord, both in Zion and Jerusalem; and third, that this Psalm was written expressly for the generation to come, and the people which shall be created shall praise the Lord, when they read it and see it fulfilled.

I will now call the attention of the reader to the first paragraph of the sixth chapter of the Record of Ether, contained in the Book of Mormon: "For he truly told them of all things from the beginning of man; and how that after the waters had receded from off the face of this land (America), it became a choice land above all other lands, a chosen land of the Lord, wherefore, the Lord would have that all men should serve Him who dwell upon the face thereof; and that it was the place of the New Jerusalem, which should come down out of heaven, and the holy sanctuary of the Lord. Behold, Ether saw the days of Christ, and he spake concerning a New Jerusalem upon this land: and he spake also concerning the house of Israel, and the Jerusalem from whence Lehi should come; after it should be destroyed, it should be built up again a holy city unto the Lord; wherefore, it could not be a New Jerusalem, for it had been in a time of old; but it should be built up again, and become a holy city of the Lord, and it should be built up unto the house of Israel; and that a New Jerusalem should be built up upon this land, unto the remnant of the seed of Joseph, for which things there has been a type; for as Joseph brought his father down into the land of Egypt, even so he died there; wherefore, the Lord brought a remnant of the seed of Joseph out of the land of Jerusalem, that He might be merciful unto the seed of Joseph, that they should perish not, even as He was merciful unto the father of Joseph, that he should perish not; wherefore, the remnant of the house of Joseph shall be built up on this land, and it shall be a land of their inheritance; and they shall build up a holy city unto the Lord, like unto the Jerusalem of old, and they shall no more be confounded, until the end come, when the earth shall pass away. And there shall be a new heaven and a new earth, and they shall be like unto the old, save the old have passed away, and all things have become new. And then cometh the New Jerusalem: and blessed are they who dwell therein, for it is they whose garments are white through the blood of the Lamb; and they are they who are numbered among the remnant of the seed of Joseph who were of the house of Israel. And then also cometh the Jerusalem of old, and the inhabitants thereof; blessed are they for they have been washed in the blood of the Lamb; and they are they who were scattered and gathered in from the four quarters of the earth, and from the north countries, and are partakers of the fulfilling of the covenant which God made with their father Abraham. And when these things come, bringeth to pass the Scripture which saith, "There are they who were first, who shall be last: and there are they who were last, who shall be first."

From this prophecy we learn—First, that America is a chosen land of the Lord, above every other land. Second, that it is the place of the New Jerusalem, which shall come down from God, out of heaven, upon the earth, when it is renewed. Third, that a New Jerusalem is to be built in America, to the remnant of Joseph, after a similar pattern, or like unto the old Jerusalem in the land of Canaan; and that the old Jerusalem shall be rebuilt at the same time, and, this being done, both cities will continue in prosperity on the earth, until the great and last change, when the heavens and the earth are to be renewed. Fourth, we learn that when this change takes place, the two cities, together with the inhabitants thereof, are to be caught up into heaven, and being changed and made new, the one comes down upon the American land, and the other to its own place as formerly: and, fifth, we learn that the inhabitants of these two cities are the same that gathered together and first builded them. The remnant of Joseph, and those gathered with them, inherit the New Jerusalem. And the tribes of Israel, gathered from the north countries, and from the four quarters of the earth, inhabit the other; and thus all things being made new, we find those who were once strangers and pilgrims on THE EARTH, in possession of that better country, and that city, for which they sought.

We will now turn to John's Revelation, and examine the city after it is made new, and see if it is anything like the pattern which it exhibited previous to its final change, Rev. xxi: "And I saw a new heaven and a new earth: for the first heaven and the first earth were passed away; and there was no more sea. And I, John, saw the holy city, New Jerusalem, coming down from God out of heaven, prepared as a bride adorned for her husband. And I heard a great voice out of heaven, saying,

Behold, the tabernacle of God is with men, and He will dwell with them, and they shall be His people, and God himself shall be with them, and be their God. And God shall wipe away all tears from their eyes; and there shall be no more death, neither sorrow, nor crying, neither shall there be any more pain: for the former things are passed away. And He that sat upon the throne said, Behold, I make all things new. And He said unto me, Write, for these words are true and faithful. And He said unto me, It is done. I am Alpha and Omega, the beginning and the end. I will give unto him that is athirst, of the fountain of the water of life freely. He that overcometh shall inherit all things; and I will be his God, and he shall be my son. But the fearful, and unbelieving, and the abominable, and murderers, and whoremongers, and sorcerers, and idolaters, and all liars, shall have their part in the lake which burneth with fire and brimstone: which is the second death.

"And there came unto me one of the seven angels which had the seven vials full of the seven last plagues, and talked with me, saying, Come hither, I will show thee the bride, the Lamb's wife. And he carried me away in the spirit to a great and high mountain, and showed me that great city, the holy Jerusalem, descending out of heaven from God, having the glory of God: and her light was like unto a stone most precious, even like a jasper stone, clear as crystal; and had a wall great and high, and had twelve gates, and at the gates, twelve angels, and names written thereon, which are the names of the twelve tribes of the children of Israel. On the east, three gates; on the north, three gates; on the south, three gates; on the west, three gates. And the wall of the city had twelve foundations, and in them the names of the twelve Apostles of the Lamb. And he that talked with me had a golden reed to measure the city, and the gates thereof, and the wall thereof. And the city lieth four square, and the length is as large as the breadth. And he measured the city with the reed, twelve thousand furlongs: the length and the breadth and the height of it are equal. And he measured the wall thereof, an hundred and forty and four cubits, according to the measure of a man, that is, of the angel. And the building of the wall of it was of jasper: and the city was of pure gold, like unto clear glass. And the foundations of the wall of the city were garnished with all manner of precious stones. The first foundation was jasper; the second, sapphire; the third, a chalcedony; the fourth, an emerald; the fifth, sardonyx; the sixth, sardius; the seventh, chrysolyte; the eighth, beryl; the ninth, a topaz; the tenth, a chrysoprasus; the eleventh, a jacinth; the twelfth, an amethyst. And the twelve gates were twelve pearls; every several gate was of one pearl: and the street of the city was pure gold, as it were transparent glass. And I saw no temple therein: for the Lord God Almighty and the Lamb are the temple of it. And the city had no need of the sun, neither of the moon, to shine in it; for the glory of God did lighten it, and the Lamb is the light thereof. And the nations of them which are saved shall walk in the light of it; and the kings of the earth do bring their glory and honor into it. And the gates of it shall not be shut at all by day; for there shall be no night there. And they shall bring the glory and honor of the nations into it. And there shall in no wise enter into it anything that defileth, neither whatsoever worketh abomination, or maketh a lie; but they which are written in the Lamb's book of life." Also, twenty-second chapter, he says: "And He showed me a pure river of water of life, clear as crystal, proceeding out of the throne of God and of the Lamb. In the midst of the street of it, and on either side of the river, was there the tree of life, which bare twelve manner of fruits, and yielded her fruit every month: and the leaves of the tree were for the healing of the nations. And there shall be no more curse: but the throne of God and of the Lamb shall be in it; and His servants shall serve Him. And they shall see His face; and His name shall be in their foreheads. And there shall be no night there; and they need no candle, neither light of the sun; for the Lord God giveth them light: and they shall reign forever and ever. And He said unto me, These sayings are faithful and true: and the Lord God of the holy prophets sent His angel to show unto His servants the things which must shortly be done. Behold, I come quickly: blessed is he that keepeth the sayings of the prophecy of this book."

From this beautiful description, we learn—First, that the new earth is not to be separated by any sea, consequently, what is now called the Eastern and Western Continents will then be one land. Secondly, we learn that the Lord will make not only the heavens and earth, but all things new (including of course, the cities of Jerusalem and Zion, where His tabernacle will have been for more than a thousand years). Thirdly, we learn that the city will lie four square, and have twelve gates, with the names of the twelve tribes of Israel, inserted, one on each gate; three gates on the north, three on the south, three on the east, and three on the west; precisely after the same manner in which it will exist temporally during the thousand years, as described by Ezekiel. Fourthly, we learn that it will be composed of precious stones, and gold, as the temporal city also will be, as described by Isaiah. Fifthly, a pure river of the water of life, clear as crystal, will flow through this renewed city, proceeding from the throne of God, just as living waters will flow from the sanctuary in the temporal city, as described by Ezekiel. Sixthly, the tree of life will stand on either side of the river, even the tree which will have once borne twelve manner of fruits, and have yielded its fruit every month, its leaves having been for the healing of the nations. But now, when John sees it, the nations have no need of healing, for there is no more death, neither pain, nor sorrow, for the former things have passed away, and all things are become new, consequently, he speaks in the past tense, and says they were for the healing of the nations; of course, referring to the times when they existed temporally, according to Ezekiel, before their final change.

Now, of the things which we have spoken this is the sum: Ezekiel and the other Prophets have presented us with the view of the cities of Zion and Jerusalem, as they will exist during the one thousand years of rest called the Millennium; and John has given us a view of the same cities, after their final change, when they come down from God out of heaven, and rest upon the new earth. But Ether has given us a sketch of them as they are to exist, both in their temporal and in their eternal state: and he has told us plainly concerning their location, first and last, namely, the New Jerusalem, in America, inhabited by the remnant of Joseph, and those gathered with them, who have washed their robes, and made them white, in the blood of the Lamb: and the other Jerusalem, in its former place, inhabited by the house of Israel gathered from the north countries, and from all countries where they were scattered, having washed their robes, and made them white, in the blood of the Lamb. And here is the end of the matter.

I would only add, that the government of the United States has been engaged, for upwards of nine years, in gathering the remnant of Joseph to the very place where they will finally build a New Jerusalem, a city of Zion, with the assistance of the Gentiles, who will gather them from all the face of the land: and this gathering is clearly predicted in the Book of Mormon, and other revelations, and the place before appointed, and the time set for its fulfilment. And except the Gentiles repent of all their abominations, and embrace the same covenant, they will soon be utterly destroyed from off the face of this land; as it is written by Isaiah: "The nation and kingdom that will not serve thee shall perish. Yea, those nations shall be utterly wasted." And as it is written by the Prophet Nephi in the Book of Mormon (n. e.), 3 Nephi, xxi:

"And, verily, I say unto you, I give unto you a sign, that ye may know the time when these things shall be about to take place, that I shall gather in from their long dispersion, my people, O house of Israel, and shall establish again among them my Zion.

"And behold, this is the thing which I will give unto you for a sign, for verily I say unto you, that when these things which I declare unto you, and which I shall declare unto you hereafter of myself, and by the power of the Holy Ghost, which shall be given unto you of the Father, shall be made known unto the Gentiles, that they may know concerning this people who are a remnant of the house of Jacob, and concerning this my people who shall be scattered by them.

"Verily, verily, I say unto you, when these things shall be made known unto them of the Father, and shall come forth of the Father, from them unto you;

"For it is wisdom in the Father that they should be established in this land, and be set up as a free people by the power of the Father, that these things might come forth from them unto a remnant of your seed, that the covenant of the Father may be fulfilled which He hath covenanted with His people, O house of Israel;

"Therefore, when these works, and the works which shall be wrought among you hereafter, shall come forth from the Gentiles, unto your seed, which shall dwindle in unbelief because of iniquity;

"For thus it behoveth the Father that it should come forth from the Gentiles, that He may shew forth His power unto the Gentiles, for this cause, that the Gentiles, if they will not harden their hearts, that they may repent and come unto me, and be baptized in my name, and know of the true points of my doctrine, that they may be numbered among my people, O house of Israel;

"And when these things come to pass, that thy seed shall begin to know these things, it shall be a sign unto them, that they may know that the work of the Father hath already commenced unto the fulfilling of the covenant which He hath made unto the people who are of the house of Israel.

"And when that day shall come, it shall come to pass that kings shall shut their mouths; for that which had not been told them shall they see; and that which they had not heard shall they consider.

"For in that day, for my sake shall the Father work a work, which shall be a great and marvellous work among them; and there shall be among them who will not believe it, although a man shall declare it unto them.

"But behold, the life of my servant shall be in my hand; therefore they shall not hurt him, although he shall be marred because of them. Yet I will heal him, for I will shew unto them that my wisdom is greater than the cunning of the devil.

"Therefore it shall come to pass, that whosoever will not believe in my words, who am Jesus Christ, whom the Father shall cause him to bring forth unto the Gentiles, and shall give unto him power that he shall bring them forth unto the Gentiles (it shall be done even as Moses said), they shall be cut off from among my people who are of the covenant.

"And my people who are a remnant of Jacob, shall be among the Gentiles, yea, in the midst of them as a lion among the beasts of the forest, as a young lion among the flocks of sheep, who, if he go through both treadeth down and teareth in pieces, and none can deliver.

"Their hand shall be lifted up upon their adversaries, and all their enemies shall be cut off.

"Yea, wo be unto the Gentiles, except they repent, for it shall come to pass in that day, saith the Father, that I will cut off thy horses out of the midst of thee, and I will destroy thy chariots,

"And I will cut off the cities of thy land, and throw down all thy strongholds;

"And I will cut off witchcrafts out of thy hand, and thou shalt have no more soothsayers;

"Thy graven images I will also cut off, and thy standing images out of the midst of thee, and thou shalt no more worship the works of thy hands;

"And I will pluck up thy groves out of the midst of thee; so will I destroy thy cities.

"And it shall come to pass that all lyings, and deceivings, and envyings, and strifes, and priestcrafts, and whoredoms, shall be done away.

"For it shall come to pass, saith the Father, that at that day whosoever will not repent and come unto my beloved Son, them will I cut off from among my people, O house of Israel;

"And I will execute vengeance and fury upon them, even as upon the heathen, such as they have not heard.

"But if they will repent, and hearken unto my words, and harden not their hearts, I will establish my Church among them, and they shall come in unto the covenant, and be numbered among this the remnant of Jacob, unto whom I have given this land for their inheritance,

"And they shall assist my people, the remnant of Jacob, and also, as many of the house of Israel as shall come, that they may build a city, which shall be called the New Jerusalem;

"And then shall they assist my people that they may be gathered in, who are scattered upon all the face of the land, in unto the New Jerusalem,

"And then shall the power of heaven come down among them; and I also will be in the midst;

"And then shall the work of the Father commence at that day, even when this Gospel shall be preached among the remnant of this people. Verily I say unto you, at that day shall the work of the Father commence among all the dispersed of my people; yea, even the tribes which have been lost, which the Father hath led away out of Jerusalem.

"Yea, the work shall commence among all the dispersed of my people, with the Father, to prepare the way whereby they may come unto me, that they may call on the Father in my name;

"Yea, and then shall the work commence, with the Father, among all nations, in preparing the way whereby His people may be gathered home to the land of their inheritance

"And they shall go out from all nations; and they shall not go out in haste, nor go by flight, for I will go before them, saith the Father, and I will be their rearward."

O ye remnant of Joseph, your secret is revealed, ye who are despised, smitten, scattered, and driven by the Gentiles from place to place, until you are left few in number! "O thou afflicted, tossed with tempest and not comforted," lift up your heads and rejoice, for your redemption draweth nigh: yea, we have found your record, the oracles of God once committed to your forefathers, which have been hidden from you for a long time, because of unbelief. Behold! they are about to be restored to you again; then shall you rejoice; for you shall know that it is a blessing from the hand of God; and the scales of darkness shall begin to fall from your eyes; and the Gentiles shall not again have power over you; but you shall be gathered by them, and be built up, and again become a delightsome people; and the time has come; yea, the work has already commenced; for we have seen you gathered together, from all parts of the land, unto the place which God has appointed for the Gentiles to gather you; therefore lay down your weapons of war, cease to oppose the Gentiles in the gathering of your various tribes, for the hand of your great God is in all this, and it was all foretold by your forefathers, ten thousand moons ago. Therefore suffer them peaceably to fulfil this last act of kindness, as a kind reward for the injuries you have received from them.

It is with mingled feelings of joy and sorrow that I reflect upon these things. Sorrow, when I think how you have been smitten; joy, when I reflect upon the happy change that now awaits you; and sorrow again, when I turn my thoughts to the awful destruction that awaits the Gentiles, except they repent. But the eternal purposes of Jehovah must roll on, until all His promises are fulfilled, and none can hinder; therefore, O God, Thy will be done! But while I still linger upon this subject, with feelings that are easier felt than described, methinks I can almost hear the Indian's mournful chant resounding through his native woods. It whispers thus:

Great Spirit of our fathers, lend an ear;

Pity the red man, to his cries give ear;

Long hast Thou scourged him with Thy chastening sore;

When will Thy vengeance cease, Thy wrath be o'er?

When will the white man's dire ambition cease,

And let our scattered remnants dwell in peace?

Or shall we, driven to the western shore,

Become extinct, and fall to rise no more?

Forbid, great Spirit! make Thy mercy known;

Reveal Thy truth; Thy wandering captives own;

Make bare Thine arm of power, for our release,

And o'er the earth extend the reign of peace.

CHAPTER VI

THE DEALINGS OF GOD WITH ALL NATIONS, IN REGARD TO REVELATION

"And hath made of one blood all nations of men for to dwell on all the face of the earth, and hath determined the times before appointed, and the bounds of their habitation; that they should seek the Lord, if haply they might feel after Him, and find Him, though He he not far from every one of us; for in Him we live, and move, and have our being." — Acts, xvii, 26-28.

In this text we learn — First, that all nations are made of one blood. Secondly, they are designed to dwell on all the face of the earth (America not excepted). Thirdly, that the Lord has determined the bounds of their habitation, that is, He has divided the earth among His children, giving each nation that portion which seemed Him good — for instance the land of Canaan, to Israel; Mount Seir, to Esau; Arabia, to Ishmael; America, to the remnant of Joseph, etc., as a father parcels off a large tract of land to his several children. And fourthly, He has granted unto all the nations of the earth the privilege of feeling after Him and finding Him; since He is not so very far from every one of them, whether they be in Asia, Africa, Europe, America, or even upon the islands of the sea. Now, if any nation, in any age of the world, or in any part of the earth, should happen to live up to their privilege, what would they obtain? I answer, revelation, for the best of reasons, because no people ever found God in any other way, nor ever will. Therefore, if they found God, they found Him by revelation, direct from Himself, He revealing His will to them; and if they did not find Him in this way, they never knew Him. And if they did obtain revelation, it was their privilege to write it, and make a record of the same, and teach it to their children; and this record would be sacred, because it would contain the word of God; and thus it would be a HOLY BIBLE, no matter whether it was written by the Jews, the Ten Tribes, the Nephites, or the Gentiles. I would just as soon have the Gospel written by Nephi, Mormon, Moroni or Alma, as the Gospel written by Matthew, Mark, Luke, or John. Again, I would just as soon believe a revelation given in America, as believe a revelation given in Asia; for if ever a nation failed to get a revelation, it was because they did not attain unto that which was their privilege But why, then, was any nation over left in darkness, from age to age, without the light of revelation to guide them? I answer, because their forefathers, in some age of the world, rejected revelation, cast out and killed the Prophets, and turned a deaf ear to the things of God, until God took away that which they enjoyed, and committed it to some other people, and left them from generation to generation to grow up in ignorance, until He should see fit again to send His light and truth to that nation; but those who reject no light are under no condemnation, and the mercy of God hath claim upon them, through the blood of Christ which atoneth for the sins of the world. The heathen who never had the light of revelation will be saved by the blood of Christ; while their forefathers who rejected the light are condemned, for this is their condemnation, that when light came they rejected it.

Now on this subject, let us examine the history of various ages. In the morn of creation, men had light by direct revelation, for Adam, Cain and Abel talked with the Lord. In the next age, men had light by revelation, for Enoch walked with the Lord, and not only saw the first coming of Christ, but His second coming also, and he exclaimed: "Behold, the Lord cometh with ten thousand of His saints, to take vengeance on the ungodly," etc., as it is written in Jude. From which it appears that Enoch knew and prophesied concerning the Messiah, with all the plainness of an Apostle. Again, in Noah's day there was positive revelation. And all these were Gentiles, or, rather, the word Israel had not yet been named upon Jacob by the angel. Now, if it was the privilege of so many Gentiles to get the word of the Lord, and to have the knowledge of the true God by revelation, it was the privilege of all the rest; and if any ran into darkness and worshiped idols, until God gave them over to work all uncleanness with greediness, and finally took the oracles of God from them, and confined them more particularly to Abraham, it was because they had for a long time rejected them, and rendered themselves unworthy of them; so that from the days of Israel the oracles of God seemed to pertain more particularly to the chosen seed, chosen for that very purpose, namely, that to them might be committed the oracles of God, the Priesthood, the service of God, and the promises which had been in existence from the beginning, among the Gentiles, who had long rendered themselves unworthy of such blessings.

But in process of time Israel rendered themselves unworthy of a continuance of such blessings, by stoning and killing the Prophets, and rejecting the Messiah, and all those that God sent unto them, until at length the Lord took the kingdom from them as a nation, and gave it again to the Gentiles; in the meantime winking at all the ignorance through which the Gentiles had passed, from the time the kingdom had been taken from them until restored again. But as soon as the kingdom of God was restored again to the Gentiles, He commanded them all everywhere to repent, and then if they did not do it they were under condemnation, but not before. But no sooner was the kingdom taken from the Jews, than the fruits of it disappeared from among them, and they were dispersed into all the nations of the earth where they have never again heard the voice of inspiration commanding them to repent. And if any Gentile has commanded them to repent and be baptized (in the name of the Lord), without being inspired and commanded to do it, it was an imposition practised upon them. Not that repentance was any harm, but the imposition consisted in professing to be sent with a message when they were not, for when God commands men to repent, He sends somebody with the command, in order that they may teach it to those for whom He designs it; and when He does not command them to do a thing, He does not require it at their hand. Any man who says that the Jews, as a nation, have been commanded to repent and be baptized, for the last seventeen hundred years, says that which he cannot prove, unless he can prove that there has been a new revelation within that time, commissioning some man to go to them with such an errand; neither will any generation of Jews, which have existed since inspiration ceased, be condemned for rejecting any message from God, for He has sent no message to them, consequently they have rejected none; but their forefathers, who did reject the things of God, are under condemnation.

Again, when men were sent with the Gospel to the Gentiles, they were commanded to repent; and this command was in force, whenever men came preaching, who were sent by proper authority, and inspired by the Holy Ghost; but when they had killed the Apostles and inspired men, and abused their privileges, until God took them away, and left them without inspiration, then the sin was answered upon that generation; and those who have since come upon the stage of action have never been commanded to repent and be baptized (except by some new revelation), and any man who says that God has commanded a Gentile to repent and obey the Gospel since the days that inspiration ceased, or since the days that Apostles and Prophets ceased from among men, says that which he will not be able to prove, unless he proves that some revelation has been given since that time, again commissioning men to go to the Gentiles with such an errand.

The fact is, God requires nothing more of a generation than to do those things which He commands them, and a generation to whom He reveals nothing, or to whom He does not send men with a message from Him, have no message to obey, and none to reject, and consequently nothing is binding on them, except the moral principles of right and wrong, which are equally binding on all ages of the world, according to the knowledge people have of moral rectitude.

But in these last days God has again spoken from the heavens, and commissioned men to go, first to the Gentiles, commanding them everywhere to repent and obey the Gospel; and then He has commanded them to go to the Jews also, and command them to repent, and obey the Gospel; thus restoring again that which has been so long lost from the earth. And wherever their voices shall be heard issuing this proclamation, in the name of Jesus, according as He has commanded them, then and there the people are under obligation to repent and be baptized. And he that repents and is baptized shall be saved; and he that does not believe their testimony, and repent and be baptized, shall be damned, for this plain reason, because God has sent them, by revelation, with this very errand, to this very generation, and they who reject the least of God's ambassadors reject Him that sent him, and therefore they are under condemnation from that time forth. But the message which God has sent these men with, is binding only on the generation to whom it is sent, and is not binding at all upon those who are dead and gone before it came; neither will it be binding on any generation which shall come after, unless God should raise up men and send unto them with the same Gospel, and then that generation to whom He sends them, will be saved or damned, according as they receive or reject their testimony.

People frequently ask this question—"If God has sent men with certain truths which are binding on the people, and without which they cannot be saved, what will become of the good people who have died before the message came?" I answer, if they obey the message which God sent to their own generation, they will be saved; but if not, they will be damned: but if God sent no message to that generation, then they rejected none, and, consequently, are under no condemnation; and they will rise up in judgment against this generation, and condemn it; for if they had received the same blessings which are now offered to us, they would no doubt have received them gladly. The principle of condemnation, in all ages of the world, is no other than rejecting the very message which God sends to them while they pretend to cleave closely to that which He has sent in former ages.

Woe unto you, Scribes and Pharisees, hypocrites! ye garnish the sepulchres of the Prophets, and say: "If we had lived in the days of our fathers, we would not have stoned and killed the Prophets as they did." But ye yourselves are witnesses, that you allow the deeds of your fathers; for they killed the Prophets, and you build their sepulchres. This was the testimony of the Savior to the Jews, who were pretending to stand stiffly for their former Prophets, and at the same time rejecting Jesus and His Apostles. And so it is now in the nineteenth century. You Christians (so called) garnish the tombs of the Messiah and His former Apostles, and even build fine chapels to their memory, entitling them Saint Peter's Church, Saint Paul's Church, Saint John's Church, etc.; and you say: "If we had lived in the days of the Apostles, we would not have stoned and killed them." But ye yourselves are witnesses, that ye allow the deeds of your fathers: for they killed the Apostles, and you build chapels in honor of them; while at the same time, if a Prophet or an Apostle comes among you, you will forthwith shut your houses against him, as soon as he testifies of what God has sent him to testify, for you say there are to be no more Prophets or Apostles on the earth, and you forthwith pronounce him a false Prophet; and if a mob rise and kill him, or burn his house, or destroy his goods, you will either rejoice, or sit in silence and give countenance to the deed, and perhaps cry, "False Prophet!" while your press and pulpits teem with all manner of lies concerning him. Woe unto you, priests, Pharisees, hypocrites! but fill ye up the measure of your fathers, for as they did, so do ye. Vengeance belongs to God. He will speedily avenge His elect, who cry unto Him day and night.

But to return to the subject of Revelation. "There is nothing secret that shall not be revealed: neither hid that shall not be known;" this was a maxim of the Savior. And again: "The knowledge of the Lord is to cover the earth, as the waters do the sea." Now, I ask how this great overturn is to be brought about? And I know no better way to answer this question, than to quote the prophecy of Nephi, Book of Mormon (n.e.), 2 Nephi, xxix, 11-14: "For I command all men, both in the east, and in the west, and in the north, and in the south, and in the islands of the sea, that they shall write the words which I speak unto them: for out of the books which shall be written, I will judge the world, every man according to their works, according to that which is written.

"For behold, I shall speak unto the Jews, and they shall write it; and I shall also speak unto the Nephites, and they shall write it; and I shall also speak unto the other tribes of the house of Israel which I have led away, and they shall write it; and I shall also speak unto all the nations of the earth, and they shall write it.

"And it shall come to pass that the Jews shall have the words of the

Nephites, and the Nephites shall have the words of the Jews; and the

Nephites and the Jews shall have the words of the lost tribes of

Israel; and the lost tribes of Israel shall have the words of the

Nephites and the Jews.

"And it shall come to pass, that my people which are of the house of Israel, shall be gathered home unto the lands of their possessions; and my word also shall be gathered in one. And I will show unto them that fight against my word, and against my people who are of the house of Israel, that I am God, and that I covenanted with Abraham, that I would remember his seed for ever."

CHAPTER VII

A CONTRAST BETWEEN THE DOCTRINE OF CHRIST AND THE DOCTRINES OF NINETEENTH CENTURY

"Whosoever transgresseth, and abideth not in the doctrine of

Christ, hath not God. He that abideth in the doctrine of Christ,

he hath both the Father and the Son." — 2 JOHN, 2.

DOCTRINE OF CHRIST.

DOCTRINES OF MEN.

And these signs shall follow them that believe.

And these signs shall not follow them that believe, for they are done away and no longer needed.

In my name shall they cast out devils.

In His name they shall not cast out devils.

They shall speak with new tongues.

The gift of tongues is no longer needed.

They shall take up serpents, and if they drink any deadly thing it shall not hurt them; they shall lay hands on the sick, and they shall recover.

If they take up serpents, they will bite them; if they drink any deadly thing it will kill them. They shall not lay hands on the sick, and if they do they shall not recover; for such things are done away.

He that believeth on me, the works that I do shall he do also; and greater works than these shall he do; because I go to the Father.

He that believeth on Christ shall not do any of the miracles and mighty works that He did, for such things have ceased.

There is nothing secret that shall not be revealed, neither hid that shall not be known.

There is to be no more revelation, for all things necessary are already revealed.

And He shall send His angels, and they shall gather His elect from the four winds, etc.

And there is to be no more ministering of angels, for such things are done away.

And I saw an angel flying in the midst of heaven, having the everlasting Gospel to preach to them that dwell on the earth, etc.

Angels do not appear in this enlightened age, because they are no longer needed.

And when He, the Spirit of Truth, is come, He will guide you into all truth; again, "He shall show you things to come."

And inspiration is no longer needed in this age of learning and refinement. Again, it shall not show you things to come: for then you would be a Prophet, and there are to be no Prophets in these days.

If ye abide in me, and my words abide in you, you shall ask what you will, in my name, and I will give it you.

It is not so in these days, we must not expect to heal the sick and work miracles, consequently we must not expect to receive what we ask for.

Father, neither pray I for these alone, but for all them that shall believe on me through their words, that they may all be one, even as we are one.

And we are all good Christians, and we all believe on Him through the

Apostles' words, although divided into several hundred sects.

One Lord, one faith, and one baptism.

Many Lords, many faiths, and three or four kinds of baptism.

And by one Spirit are ye all baptized into one body.

And by many spirits are we all torn asunder into different bodies.

And God gave some Apostles; and some, Prophets; and some, Evangelists; and some, Pastors and Teachers; for the perfecting of the Saints, for the work of the ministry, for the edifying of the body of Christ.

And there are to be no more Apostles, and no more Prophets. But the work of the ministry, the perfecting of the Saints, and the edifying of the different bodies of Christ, can all be done very well without these gifts of God, only give us money enough to educate and employ the wisdom of men.

These gifts and offices were to continue until we all come into the unity of the faith, and of the knowledge of the Son of God, unto a perfect man, unto the measure of the stature of the fulness of Christ.

Apostles, miracles and gifts were to continue during the first age of Christianity, and then were to cease, because no longer needed, having accomplished their purpose.

These gifts and offices were given that we henceforth be no more children, tossed to and fro, and carried about with every wind of doctrine, by the sleight of men, and cunning craftiness, whereby they lie in wait to deceive.

Tracts, creeds, sermons and commentaries of uninspired men, together with a hireling priesthood, are now necessary in order to keep men from being carried about with every wind of doctrine, etc.

For no man taketh this honor unto himself, but he that is called of

God, as was Aaron.

For no man taketh this honor unto himself, but one who has been educated for the purpose, and commissioned by men.

But how shall they preach, except they be sent (of God)?

But how shall they preach except they be well educated for the purpose, and sent (by the board of officers)?

Is any sick among you? let him call for the Elders of the Church; and let them pray over him, anointing him with oil in the name of the Lord: and the prayer of faith shall save the sick, and the Lord shall raise him up; and if he have committed sins they shall be forgiven him.

If any are sick among you, do not send for the Elders of the Church; or, if the Elders come, do not let them lay hands on them, neither let them anoint them in the name of the Lord, for this is all "Mormon" delusion, but send for a good physician, and perhaps they may get well.

Repent and be baptized every one of you in the name of Jesus Christ, for the remission of sins, and ye shall receive the gift of the Holy Ghost; for the promise is unto you, and to your children, and to all that are afar off, even as many as the Lord our God shall call.

Repent and come to the anxious seat (penitent form), every one of you, and cry, "Lord, Lord," and may be you will get forgiveness of sins; and you may be baptized or not; but if you do, you will not get the Holy Ghost as they did anciently, for such things are done away.

It shall come to pass in the last days, saith God, that I will pour out my Spirit upon all flesh: and your sons and your daughters shall prophesy, and your young men shall see visions, and your old men shall dream dreams; etc.

And in these last days the Lord will not pour out His Spirit so as to cause our sons and daughters to prophesy, our old men to dream dreams, and our young men to see visions; for such things are no longer needed, and it is all a delusion, and none but the ignorant believe such things.

Covet earnestly the best gifts, but rather that ye prophesy.

Do not covet any of the supernatural gifts, but especially beware of prophesying, for such things are done away.

Covet to prophesy, and forbid not to speak with tongues.

Do not prophesy, and it is all a delusion to speak in tongues.

But in vain do they worship me, teaching for doctrines the commandments of men.

It matters not what kind of doctrine, or what system, a man embraces, if he is only sincere and worships Jesus Christ.

I thank thee, O Father, Lord of heaven and earth, because thou hast hid these things from the wise and prudent, and hast revealed them unto babes; even so, Father, for so it seemed good in thy sight.

We thank God that He has revealed nothing to any person, wise or simple, for many hundred years, but that our wise and learned men have been able to know God without a revelation, and that we shall never be favored with any more.

No man knoweth the Son but the Father, neither knoweth any man the

Father save the Son, and he to whomsoever the Son will reveal Him.

We all know God in this enlightened age, and yet neither the Father nor the Son has revealed any thing to any of us, for we do not believe revelations are necessary now.

And this is life eternal, that they might know Thee the only true God, and Jesus Christ, whom Thou hast sent.

And we cannot know for ourselves, by any positive manifestation, in these days, but must depend on the wisdom and learning of men.

I thank my God always on your behalf, for the grace of God which is given you by Jesus Christ, that in everything ye are enriched by Him in all utterance, and in all knowledge, even as the testimony of Christ (the spirit of prophecy) was confirmed in you, so that ye come behind in no good gift, waiting for the coming of our Lord Jesus Christ.

We thank the Lord always, in behalf of the Church in these days, that she has no supernatural gifts given unto her, and that she is not enriched by Christ, neither in the gift of utterance, nor in the gift of knowledge; neither has she the testimony of Jesus (the spirit of prophecy) confirmed in her, and she comes behind in all the gifts; nor is she waiting for, or expecting, the coming of the Lord; for He has come once, and never will come again till the great and last day, the end of the earth.

The foolishness of God is wiser than men; and the weakness of God is stronger than men. For you see your calling, brethren, how that not many wise men after the flesh, not many mighty, not many noble, are called: but God hath chosen the foolish things of the world to confound the wise; and God hath chosen the weak things of the world to confound the things which are mighty, and base things of the world, and things which are despised, hath God chosen; yea, and things which are not, to bring to nought things that are; that no flesh should glory in His presence.

The wisdom of men, and the learning of men, are better than the inspiration of the Almighty, for that is not needed any longer; for you see your calling, brethren, how that the wise and learned, and noble, and mighty are called in these days; for we have chosen such to confound the foolish, the unlearned, and the ignorant; yea, to confound the base things of the world which are despised, that flesh might glory in His presence.

And I, brethren, when I came to you, came not with excellency of speech or of wisdom, declaring unto you the testimony of God; for I determined not to know anything among you, save Jesus Christ and Him crucified. And I was with you in weakness, and in fear, and in much trembling. And my speech and my preaching was not with enticing words of man's wisdom, but in demonstration of the Spirit and of power; that your faith should not stand in the wisdom of men, but in the power of God.

And we, brethren, when we came unto you, came with excellency of speech, and with the wisdom and learning of man; and our speech and our preaching were with enticing words of man's wisdom, not in demonstration of the Spirit and power, for that is done away; that your faith should not stand in the power of God, but in the wisdom of man.

But we speak the wisdom of God in a mystery, even the hidden wisdom, which God ordained before the world unto our glory; which none of the princes of this world knew: for had they known it, they would not have crucified the Lord of glory.

But we speak the wisdom of man in a mystery, even the hidden wisdom which none but the learned knew; for had others known it, they would never have been under the necessity of employing us to tell it to them.

But God hath revealed them unto us, by His Spirit; for the Spirit searcheth all things, yea, the deep things of God.

But God hath revealed nothing unto us by His Spirit; for the wisdom and learning of man search all things; yea, all the deep things which are necessary for us to know.

For what man knoweth the things of a man, save the spirit of man which is in him? Even so the things of God knoweth no man, but the Spirit of God.

For what man knoweth the things of man, save the spirit of man, which is in him? even so the things of God knoweth no man by the Spirit of God in these days, for it is done away, or it reveals nothing.

Now we have received not the spirit of the world, but the Spirit which is of God: that we might know the things that are freely given to us of God.

Now we have not received the Spirit of God, but the spirit of the world, that we might not know for a certainty, but that we might guess at, or give our opinion of, the things of God.

Which things also we speak, not in the words which man's wisdom teacheth, but which the Holy Ghost teacheth: comparing spiritual things with spiritual.

Which things also we speak, not in the words which the Holy Ghost teacheth, but which man's wisdom teacheth; for the inspiration of the Holy Ghost is done away.

But the natural man receiveth not the things of the Spirit of God: for they are foolishness unto him; neither can he know them, because they are spiritually discerned.

But the learned man may receive and understand the things of God by his own wisdom, without the inspiration of the Spirit; for who will be so foolish as to believe in visions and revelations in this religious age?

Let no man deceive himself. If any man among you seemeth to be wise in this world, let him become a fool, that he may be wise.

Let no man deceive himself. If any man among you seemeth to be wise in the things of God, let him get the wisdom of men, that he may be wise.

For the wisdom of this world is foolishness with God: for it is written, He taketh the wise in their own craftiness. And again, The Lord knoweth the thoughts of the wise, that they are vain. Therefore, let no man glory in men.

For the wisdom of God is foolishness with the world, for it is written, Let us educate young men for the ministry; and again, Let no man preach who has not been educated for the purpose; and especially, receive no man who professes to be inspired.

Now concerning spiritual gifts, brethren, I would not have you ignorant.

Now, concerning spiritual gifts, brethren, we would have you entirely ignorant, for they are not needed at all in this generation.

But the manifestation of the Spirit is given to every man to profit withal.

But the manifestation of the Spirit is given to no man to profit at all.

For to one is given by the Spirit the word of wisdom; to another, the word of knowledge by the same Spirit.

But to one is given, by the learning of men, the word of wisdom; and to another, the word of knowledge by human learning.

To another, faith by the same Spirit; to another, the gifts of healing by the same Spirit.

And to another, faith, by the same Spirit; but to none the gift of healing by the same Spirit.

To another, the working of miracles; to another, prophecy; to another, discerning of spirits; to another, divers kinds of tongues; to another, the interpretation of tongues.

And to none the working of miracles, and to none to prophesy; and to none discerning of spirits; and to none to speak with divers kinds of tongues, and to none to interpret tongues.

For as the body is one, and hath many members, and all the members of that one body, being many, are one body, so also is Christ.

For as the body is composed of many sects and parties who are opposed to each other, and have no gifts, and being many sects, are but one body, so also is Antichrist.

For by one Spirit are we all baptized into one body, whether we be Jews or Gentiles, whether we be bond or free; and have been all made to drink into one Spirit.

For by many spirits are we all baptized into many bodies, whether we be Catholics or Protestants, Presbyterians or Methodists, but have all drunk into one spirit, even the spirit of the world.

For the body is not one member, but many.

For the body is not one sect, but many.

But now hath God set the members every one of them in the body, as it hath pleased Him.

But now hath the God (of this world) set the sects and parties in the body (of Antichrist) as it hath pleased him.

And if they were all one member, where were the body?

And if they were all one sect, where were the body?

But now are they many members, but one body.

But now are they many sects, yet but one body (even Babylon).

Now ye are the body of Christ, and members in particular.

Now ye are the body of Antichrist, and members in particular.

And God hath set some in the Church: first, Apostles; secondly, Prophets; thirdly, Teachers; after that, miracles; then, gifts of healings, helps, governments, diversities of tongues.

And man hath set some in the church, first, a hireling priest; secondly, a board of officers; thirdly, tracts; then commentaries, creeds, and diversities of opinions; hence, societies and wondrous helps.

Blessed are ye, when men shall revile you, and persecute you, and shall say all manner of evil against you falsely, for my sake: rejoice, and be exceeding glad; for great is your reward in heaven; for so persecuted they the Prophets which were before you.

Woe unto you, when men revile you, and persecute you, and say all manner of evil against you falsely for Christ's sake. Lament ye, and be exceedingly sorrowful in that hour, for little is your reward among men, for so persecute they the Latter-day Saints.

Give to him that asketh thee; and from him that would borrow of thee turn thou not away.

Give to him that asketh of thee, if he be able to make thee a similar present; and from him that would borrow of thee turn not thou away, if he be able to pay thee again with good interest.

Be ye therefore perfect even as your Father who is in heaven is perfect.

Do not think to be perfect, for it is impossible to live without sin.

Take heed that you do not your alms before men, to be seen of them; otherwise ye have no reward of your Father who is in heaven.

Take heed that you do your alms before men, to be seen of them; otherwise, you have no reward nor praise from the children of men.

Therefore, when thou doest thine alms, do not sound a trumpet before thee, as the hypocrites do in the synagogues and in the streets, that they may have glory of men. Verily I say unto you, They have their reward.

Therefore when thou doest thine alms, publish it in the Missionary

Herald, or some other paper, that you may get praise of the world.

Verily I say unto you, You shall have your reward.

And when thou prayest, thou shalt not be as the hypocrites are; for they love to pray standing in the synagogues and in the corners of the streets, that they may be seen of men.

And when thou prayest, be like the hypocrites in days of old; go before the public and cry mightily, not expecting to be heard and answered, for that would be miraculous, and miracles have ceased.

Moreover, when ye fast, be not, as the hypocrites, of a sad countenance: for they disfigure their faces, that they may appear unto men to fast. Verily I say unto you, They have their reward.

Moreover, when ye fast, be like the hypocrites, of a sad countenance, that ye may appear unto men to fast; so that you may get your reward.

Lay not up for yourselves treasures upon earth, where moth and rust doth corrupt, and where thieves break through and steal: but lay up for yourselves treasures in heaven, where neither moth nor rust doth corrupt, and where thieves do not break through nor steal; for where your treasure is, there will your heart be also.

Lay up for yourselves abundance of treasures on the earth, where moth and rust doth corrupt, and where thieves break through and steal; for if your heart is only in heaven, it is no matter how rich you are in this world; for now it is come to pass that ye can serve God and mammon.

Therefore all things whatsoever ye would that men should do to you, do ye even so to them: for this is the law and the Prophets.

Therefore all things whatsoever men do to you, do ye even so to them; for this is the law and the practice.

Enter ye in at the straight gate; for wide is the gate, and broad is the way, that leadeth to destruction, and many there be which go in thereat.

Enter ye in at the wide gate, where the multitude go: for it cannot be that all our great and learned men are wrong, and nobody right but a few obscure individuals.

Because straight is the gate, and narrow is the way, that leadeth unto life, and few there be that find it.

For the narrow way is not altogether too straight, but only a very few travel in it.

Beware of false prophets, which come to you in sheep's clothing, but inwardly they are ravening wolves. Ye shall know them by their fruits. Do men gather grapes of thorns, or figs of thistles?

Beware of Prophets who come to you with the Word of God; you may know at once they are false, without hearing them or examining their fruits; popular opinion is against them; whereas, if they were men of God, the people would speak well of them.

Wherefore, by their fruits ye shall know them. Not every one that saith unto me, Lord, Lord, shall enter into the kingdom of heaven; but he that doeth the will of my Father who is in heaven.

If we are only sure that we have experienced religion, and we pray often, we shall be saved, whether we do the Lord's will or not; for it mattereth not what system we embrace, whether it be right or wrong, if we are only sincere.

And it came to pass, when Jesus had ended these sayings, the people were astonished at His doctrine: for He taught them as one having authority, and not as the scribes.

And it came to pass, when men had ended these sayings, the people were pleased with their doctrines, for they taught them not as men having authority, but as the scribes.